Fundraising

For the Small Community

An in-depth, hands-on, how-to book

Kelvin B. Kent

ISBN 0-7414-1568-2

Published by:

INFINITY
PUBLISHING.COM

519 West Lancaster Avenue
Haverford, PA 19041-1413
Info@buybooksontheweb.com
www.buybooksontheweb.com
Toll-free (877) BUY BOOK
Local Phone (610) 520-2500
Fax (610) 519-0261

Printed in the United States of America

Printed on Recycled Paper

Published July 2003

CONTENTS

Dedication i
Acknowledgments ii
Introduction 1
This Book in One Page 5
Understanding the basics 6
Starting out small 12
Organization that works 14
The Art of Solicitation 20
Understanding the Perspective of the Small Business Donor 29
Putting on an Event 34
The Silent Auction 43
The Annual Fundraiser 49
    Annual Membership 50
    Annual Traditional Method 53
    The Non Event 53
    The Golf Tournament 54
    The Major Auction and/or Garage Sale 58
    The Sponsored Event 66
    The Jail or Lock Up 68
    The Fundraising Dinner 71
    Raffles 72
    The Silent Auction 76
    The Salon 79
    Other Events 81
    Memorials 83
    Final Thoughts Concerning Annual Fundraising 84
Letterheads and Logos 86
The Major Capital Project 90
Churches 116
Grants 126
501(c)(3)Organizations 140
    Foundations 145
    Endowments themselves 148
Professional Consultants and Organizers 151
Saying "Thank You" 154
Conclusion 157
Examples of Fundraising Tools 159

This book is dedicated to Clifford E. Baldridge

A man who led by example
and always took out his own checkbook first

Acknowledgments

It was my wife Becky who suggested that I do this. We were on a hike in the San Juan Mountains of Western Colorado and I was recovering from heart surgery. I think it was her way of getting me to become more proficient on our computer by jotting down some of what I had enjoyed doing for many years!

I didn't exactly feel I needed one more consuming task because of other events in my life, (including the production of two local hiking guides and the start of a third one). But I did allow myself to become fascinated with the idea of sharing the expertise that a number of people thought I had. And, so now, with this completed work, I thank Becky for her foresight and encouragement.

For certain sections I have enlisted the aid of local friends who have guided me in the right direction. Curtis Robinson, a retired CPA and one of the finest community leaders and manager of funds I have had the honor to know, and Dana Burns CPA with Dalby Wendland and Co, both offered assistance on the subject of 501(c)(3)) organizations. Lynda Alfred, local yoga teacher and semi professional grant writer, gave me some good advice, which supplemented and improved what I had produced. Greg Crippen kindly shared his consummate knowledge in organizing highly successful and income-producing golf tournaments. Kristin Redmond saved me lots of time by downloading oodles of documents relating to raffles. Eva Preslan, Leon Brestel and Vickie Wilson all rescued me from various computer dilemmas.

Rebecca Salinger, down in Austin, Texas, most graciously agreed to do some laborious work in proof reading and help with format. Rebecca is actually my sister-in-law and her professional knowledge in this field made me understand how little I knew about it.

My last acknowledgement is to my local community, centered around Montrose, Colorado. Montrose is a special place that I have known since 1976. It is clean, beautiful, small enough to be perfect for raising a family but large enough to provide cultural and other facilities more befitting a community of twice its size. It is close to the mountains, fishing and hunting, has a great climate and attracts wonderful people. But most important of all, it is a community that understands that fundraising and contributing to its own infrastructure is a part of its spirit. Indeed, there are literally hundreds of tangible results ranging from our beautiful Pavilion (combined senior center, performing arts auditorium, community center and meeting and banquet facility), new award winning library, wonderful aquatic center, state of the art high school gymnasium and track, to a world-class skateboard park, highly successful Hospice program, active Habitat for Humanity group and so many more smaller facilities and services from which we all benefit.

Motivating people, including ourselves, to give, produces wonderful returns. Montrose has given me more than I can ever repay. My thanks go to everyone.

(All quotes shown in the boxes at the beginning of each chapter,
except for the chapter on Churches,
are those of the author.)

Introduction

All forms of giving bless the giver. This includes the raising of money to help a good cause or benefit others. The cup that we are given doesn't just fill up; it tends to overflow to the extent that we are given a larger cup. Many great figures over the centuries have indicated that the most satisfying state in life, and attainment of lasting happiness, come from the rendering of service to those whose need is greater than ours. I know this to be true and encourage everyone to share in these rewards.

Helping to raise money in one form or another has been a part of my life. I remember, back in my little island of Jersey, in the British-owned Channel Islands, close to Normandy, being asked to join in the cub scouts "bob a job week." I must have been about 8 at the time but I innately knew that raising money was connected with service and that service was a duty to mankind. We were doing something for others as, indeed, throughout life, they would do for us. In those days a bob was slang for a shilling, which is about 5 pence or a dime now. We would rake leaves for 3 hours or stack wood or sweep clean a driveway or (hand) mow a lawn. It didn't matter how long it took. It was the satisfaction of completing a task and getting paid for it. The difference was that, depending on how we did it and our attitude, what we got would frequently be more than a bob. Sometimes we got two bob or even ten bob. And at the end of the week, we would all go into the scout building with our list and bag of coins and see how we'd done. Some kids only managed 2 or 3 jobs and even these were with their folks or close relatives. I was able to get 30 jobs and win (for all of us), the biggest contribution. There were reasons for this. First, I would visit a mixture of houses and on some of them (especially the bigger ones), I would ask if they had a big job that they had put off doing but that we could help them with. If the answer was yes, I'd race back home and get my brother and we'd both go. The result was often amazing. It turned out that although they were paying us with good money (and cookies), it was their very real perception that we were doing them the favor and not vice-versa. We made them feel good!

Later, as a student in London, there were constant opportunities to help raise money for worthwhile causes like the YMCA or to assist fellow employees or students whose misfortune prevented them from having the money to pay for a fare home for Christmas.

Even in the Army, serving with Gurkha troops from Nepal, we would devise methods to raise funds for their Welfare Trust and get money to families who had lost everything in the Indian monsoon. Sometimes there would be a need like a play or swing set for the young kids. I'd form a camera club, even buying a couple of old second-hand cameras and produce reasonable quality pictures which we sold to everyone on the base to send home to their families. In places like Borneo and Sarawak, these pics were not like your normal postcards! The point is that we learned to use one source of manpower to provide what another segment didn't have.

Perhaps all of this is more about a sense of involvement; of realizing that we're not put on this earth to merely receive. But, instead, one of our purposes is to join, to help equalize, to look with compassion on others who have less and to address unmet needs. From this comes the notion that small communities grow and prosper because of what we all contribute to them. What sort of need is there? How can we meet it? Note that the "we" here, is not and should not be "how can the government give us everything we want." Of course, there are exceptions. Persuading the city fathers that a half percent sales tax increase is a good way to go to help fund our community center may be acceptable. But even here, the qualification that it should only be for a finite period and sunsetted afterwards, is empathetic and prudent.

And as with all other fundraising, even a measure like this requires a strong representation of the need, and an ability to sell the concept in such a way that a majority will support it by voting "yes" on the ballot. After all, it is their money and it will be their decision as to how they prioritize the spending of it.

And so to this book. After well over 50 years of trying to do my part, and receiving in return, a wonderful sense of belonging and so many rewards that are completely beyond the odd plaque, I came to the conclusion that my best contribution to this so-called "art" would be to jot down some of what I have and continue to learn. I hope that I am not setting myself up as an expert so much as to do my best to save some time for others. I have attempted to do this in a practical, simple and down to earth fashion.

Although it has been my desire to take a lot of acquired knowledge and place it all it into a logical sequence, I realize that there is bound to be overlap. Much of this is intentional because it would be overwhelming to put every little nugget of advice into one particular section. I have not, therefore made each of the sections necessarily complete in themselves. For some, I've thrown in a number of pertinent techniques and tips and to others, I've done much the same but listed these techniques from a different viewpoint, together with other thoughts. Many such kernels are shown only once. My intention has been to spread a broad base of practical knowledge over the entire course of the book, while still being specific in many instances. Most of the deep down principles apply to every aspect and level of fundraising and nearly all of them can be applied in a cross-over fashion.

That is why, if you have got this far, I hope that you will read the whole thing and make your own notes, before leaping up to enthuse others with your next fundraising project. And if you find an error or would like to send me something for inclusion in the next edition, please do so. I will be honored.

My contact address is:
Kelvin Kent
PO Box 583
Ouray, Colorado 81427
Email: beckykelvin@ocinet.net

If anyone can benefit just a little bit from this endeavor, then I will have succeeded and be happy. But as you will see over and over again, to read something is one thing; to do it is another. **So do, ask and receive!**

This Book in One Page

Here is the nub of this book

1. Establish the cause.
2. Reconcile the need.
3. Recruit a proven fundraising leader.
4. Set example by giving first.
5. Ask.
6. Receive.
7. Thank everybody.

And here is the bottom line

The Nike slogan sums it up: "Just do it!" There is no magic formula. There is no fairy godmother. Fundraising is hard work. Talking about it is one thing. Doing it is another.

It is both an art and a science. It takes a lot of time. It takes dedication and it takes follow through.

The reward always makes it worthwhile. Helping others to benefit and achieve a result that, otherwise, would not happen, defines the highest order of service to and for your community.

Enthusiasm, optimism, energy, integrity and sound motivational characteristics are the qualities needed to make it happen. Out of this is derived deep satisfaction and the type of leadership approval that is earned through example and the recognition of others on the team.

Understanding the basics

Fundraising is always a learning experience in relationships. It starts with making a strong effort to understand other people's perspectives and ends with giving them an invitation to respond.

Just before I finished getting this book ready to send to the publisher, a good friend of mine called me and asked me to help out with the annual local Boy Scouts of America appeal. We met together at a church hall to collect our packets and prospect lists. The Boy Scout paid coordinator was there and coffee and donuts were served. There were even attractive brochures about the world of scouting. But what was missing for me were selling statistics. What I wanted to know were facts like how many scouts there were in our district? Where were the troops located? How many Eagle Scouts were there and how many more were being trained? Exactly how did our local scouts benefit from the money being raised? Where did it go and how much needed to be raised?

Only after I got all of these questions answered, did I feel that I could confidently start to solicit from individuals and businesses in our area. The fact that scouting is a worthy cause was not, by itself enough. I had to have the facts which enabled me to buy in sufficiently myself, to convince others of the need.

In going round to my various prospects, one business owner who I knew quite well said something like: "Oh no! I suppose you've got your hand out for money again? "Yes" I replied, "you don't get much result without doing that."

Fundraising is an undertaking that few people volunteer for. It involves many different talents and characteristics, including organizational skills, math, understanding people, ability to motivate, timing, and personal example. But above all, fundraising at the grass roots level requires goal setting and hard work. There is no substitute for this. None.

Make no mistake, even with all of the modern technology available, getting money from someone else is never easy, never to be taken for granted and seldom achieved without being able to present a strong case, in writing, and/or verbally, on a one to one basis. In reality, whatever the cause and however important it may be, all fundraising should be considered a special interest. In the larger realm of things, the particular cause, valid as it may be, represents only a very small fraction of all the other ongoing and unmet needs of any given community. In the eyes of the giver, it may be seen as anything from "useful" to "totally irrelevant." The sad truth is that, like it or not, you have to make your cause appear more important than everyone else's!

But be careful; everyone else's cause is still important and whether or not you personally support these other causes, (that are often in competition with yours), is not the issue. Just don't knock them. Don't try to convince potential donors that others are a waste of time and never criticize the efforts or cause of another individual or organization who is trying their best to do exactly what you are doing for their special interest. The fact is that in any community, there exists a diverse population with a broad spectrum of interests and priorities. For instance, the need for an improvement to a county fairground or additional funding for the Ducks Unlimited organization or support for a dialysis machine or raising funds to bring in a world famous chamber music trio will no doubt not be supported by all of the same people. Some, who are natural givers, may give to all or perhaps three out of the four. A lot of others will possibly support one and not the rest. Still others won't feel that it is their responsibility to help with any of them.

Unfortunately, a huge percentage of the local population just does not give, in the sense of being seen to support community causes. But those same people may, in fact, be giving most generously to their churches or helping out a family member in need or they may feel that saving for a child's education is the single most giving thing they should be doing right now. Others suffer from a scarcity mentality. They feel that by giving, they will end up with less. Most natural givers know that this is not so. But it is still hard to convince some people that helping a local cause is both rewarding psychologically as well as providing the opportunity to become involved with something that is greater than themselves. They are not even aware of the blessings they deny through not becoming open to the concept of giving and receiving. Perhaps this is for selfish reasons and perhaps it is because they are loners and don't feel that they belong, or even want to. Frequently this group is either virtually unapproachable or will quickly produce numerous reasons for why the cause should not be supported, least of all, by people like themselves.

If we can move them to see the need, become involved, contribute, and share in the blessing, both they and we will have bridged the gap of greater understanding. They become a donor. They become "inspired." We have merely opened a door for them and shown them a beautiful garden beyond.

Fundamentals

We can talk all we want to about fundraising, the types of people who do it best, and the techniques involved. We can read dozens of books that seek to suggest that all is possible. We can set goals to reach and we can spend time in endless discussion about who we think will contribute, but in the end, it all boils down to this:

1. We want to extract money from others.
2. These "others" already have lots of things to do with their money.
3. These "others" are often us. And if they're not, they're not much different from most of us.
4. We have to create in them a good reason to part with their money and give it to us.
5. We have to ask.

It is generally understood by a lot of people that all giving is reciprocated. Therefore, we have to feel good about performing the role of creating, for another person, **a giving opportunity**.

Understanding that there is always much good pleasure to be derived from the act of giving is crucial to the person who is asking. Some people have never experienced this and are unaware of the rewards.

And so, asking for money is a most honorable undertaking. Money is not a dirty word. Its what makes our world go round and pays for nearly everything that benefits others. It is as important a resource as time and equally to be respected. Getting money from those who can and want to give, as well as from those who are more reluctant, is the finest form of recycling.

This book's aim is to get us to see that fundraising is essential for any worthwhile program to work and that cash and in-kind contributions are indispensable for any capital project to start. Most people understand this basic principle but most people don't want to do the actual work of raising money. But they do know that someone will step up to do it and, deep down, they are most grateful that it is you and not them. In fact, most people who have been around for some time will tell you that they are extremely relieved and truly appreciate you for performing that role.

Fundraising is action. It is doing. It is out on the street. It is meeting people. It is willing to face rejection. It is time consuming. It is selfless. But it is as fine a service to humanity and the community as anything else can be and it is completely rewarding. It is the one element of a project or endeavor, without which nothing else can be achieved.

It is not a "you" or "I" thing. It is a "we" thing. A win win and an act of love, which requires courage, determination, belief in what you're doing and commitment to the cause and goal.

Media

Without positive media support, any fundraiser will fall short of its maximum potential. Although it may often be preferential to use the more friendly pro-active media, no one should be omitted. It therefore becomes very important to compile a comprehensive media database, which includes the following:

Newspapers

- Name of publication, address, telephone number and Email address.
- Publisher, editor, feature reporter and community announcement person.
- Days of publishing and deadlines.
- Not for profit display rates.

Radio

- Name of station(s), and company name.
- Owner, General manager, News director.
- Not for profit spot rates.
- Same details for public radio stations.

TV

- Same as for radio.

Also include, on this list, any other publications, newsletters, calendars etc, which publish local events. These may include chambers of commerce, city, county, senior citizens organizations and others. Bear in mind, also, that neighboring towns and communities may have their own media and regional calendars, some of which cover your community.

PSAs are public service announcements. All media have to allocate space or time to provide a mandated number of these spots. They can be very useful tools to use if you know how they work. They nearly always require certain criteria to be met and do have to be submitted well in advance. "Camera ready" submissions can be an advantage and so, too, can voice-overs by someone well known and recognized in the community. Try to make them eye catching or audibly appealing and enticing. Be creative and get to know the media people concerned. Many will go the extra mile to help if they know you have respect for their work and provide something that is not dull and uninteresting.

Starting out small

> 80% of something is better than 100% of nothing. To wait for everything to be perfect is to tacitly agree that this project will never get off the ground.

Fundraising can be done at several different levels. One of the aims has to be to make it personal. For example, if a young woman at school gets selected to go to State for something like a Miss Teen pageant, she may have to raise $1,000 or so to be able to go. Where does she start?

Well, as in nearly all echelons of fundraising, she will probably start with her own family and immediate circle of friends, especially adults. In this particular case, a letter probably won't produce much, even though she should have some data and "official looking" information which supports her claim. But when it comes down to it, this type of effort can hardly be said to be of tangible benefit to the community, unless she can persuade people that it is! So a classical technique is called for. She must base her request and approach, not on her own natural beauty or accomplishments, but on how much she wants to represent her town or community and that she is working hard to beat all others so that she can bring home the prize for "this town." Now, it becomes more meaningful. She has shifted the attention from herself to the community. She will still have to sell herself and talents, but the reasons for doing so will be directed towards the benefits of others. No one can do this selling for her. She will still have to learn how to present herself in such a fashion as to garner assistance. Even before going out to solicit funds, she should try to arrange a print media story, complete with photo. She should have plenty of copies available to show and hand out. She should know, to whom checks should be written and have a little receipt pad. Above all, she should know what the goal is and when she wants to accomplish it by.

Having already earned support from family, she will need to rehearse a short speech, which equates to the following: "I've worked so hard. I think I have a good chance of placing well in this pageant and my goal is to win! I would be so proud to do this for my community and I've already got pledges and have raised $350 towards the $1000 costs involved. I'm hoping you will support me in my desire to do well for our community." Lastly, she needs to know what to ask for. If she goes for $100 it may well be too much and just not affordable or reconcilable in the mind of the donor but if she says something like: "I'm trying to get as many of our local businesses as possible involved and participating with me and I'm looking for contributions of $25 or $30, or more if you feel you are able, but really, I'd rather just have $10 or $15 from you than suggest too much. I think I'd like to leave the amount up to you."

If this sounds like a little fairy tale, it is. But, as with all such tales, there is much to be learned and this girl's beauty pageant is still only a dream unless she can actually get there to compete. Lets hope she does well and remembers to thank those who helped make it possible for her because this final act will determine the response given to the next girl who comes along.

Organization that works

> It is essential to formulate a plan, enthuse other people with it, motivate them to participate and, with the combination of gentleness and firmness, make them accountable for doing their part to help ensure a joint completion of the goal.

For any fundraising endeavor to be successful, the key pre-requisite has to be the example set by the board. If the board is not passionate and motivated and totally supportive, the whole venture is likely to fizzle out. And when I say board, I mean all of them. There cannot be any feeling of opposition, or worse still, a split-off section that ends up in sabotaging the project. If compromises have to be made, that is OK, but let all of that happen before the fundraising program starts, because after it does, it is essential that the whole board be united.

If, at any time, the purpose, timings and financial goal have not been clearly stated, go back to the (drawing!) board and obtain clarification. Make sure that supporting facts and figures are in place. If there is a design involved, conceptual diagrams are important. In other words, make sure you have all the tools necessary to do the job. It is not considered the fundraising committee's function to be the visionary or the architect of the project. But it is the fundraising committee head's job to become involved in the setting of the financial goal. In the mind of the person who is heading the fundraising effort, this goal has to be realistic, achievable and reconcilable.

Assuming that all of the above are in place and that everyone on the board has already written their check or pledged a suitable sum of money, the next step is to form a fundraising committee. The choice of individuals is crucial. Most of them must be willing to solicit and be capable of selling. People like real estate agents or retail sales people are naturally good but so too are managerial people who have out-going personalities. Generally speaking the most effective ones are those who are achievement orientated. But there is also a need for a couple of reliable and detailed minded people to handle some of the administrative aspects of the effort. Try to look for positive, cheerful, confident men and women who respond to a good challenge and enjoy coming through.

Some thoughts on the committee and its leadership

"I'm not good at asking for money!" How often have we heard that one? It is nothing more than a weak cop-out and it is unacceptable. Excluding pure grace and the unconditional love that we should all show for each other, everything we want has to be asked for. We ask for a raise, children ask for a bicycle or a vehicle, we ask for a commitment from others. Why, therefore, can we not ask someone to support our cause? Note, though, that the term "our cause" is only ours in the sense that we are performing a task on other people's behalf. They should be grateful! The cause itself is really the community's cause or at least, a good segment of the community's. In all cases, it is one which benefits others, beyond ourselves. Nothing, therefore, could be more honorable or of more service than to seek funds to provide something that is needed. And keep in mind that many great people throughout history have come to the conclusion that service of this kind and looking to the needs for others ultimately provides the single greatest source of personal happiness.

Lets start with the fundraising leader. We have stated the traits required elsewhere so lets just assume that he or she has an impressive track record and fits the bill. Quite possibly this leader will be a strong personality and a real "go getter." Their temperament might also be a little threatening to some. They will probably be sharp thinkers and be used to moving at a fast pace. They may not like to waste time and they may even tend to be somewhat autocratic. Like it or not, these qualities should be considered acceptable and allowances made for this type of management style. In fact, the idea of consensus rarely enters their minds because they know that this approach leads to delays, tabling of important decision-making and a slowing down of the process. Worse still, it can result in a watering down of key wording in letters or methods of approach. This is not to say that consensus is not desirable. It merely means that it is difficult to achieve and may result in the leader losing interest or working against his or her better judgment. Ideally, these things should all be ironed out early on. In fact, a good board or director should dedicate a major portion of a meeting agenda (or convene a special meeting), solely to the subject of fundraising. The board should formally accept the nomination for fundraising chair and discuss the parameters under which that chair operates, taking into account his/her preferences and proposed mode of operendum. This is the one and only time that all parties should be convinced that the right choice has been made and that the fundraising leader is well and truly "sold" on the project. Any objections or reservations that he or she may have must be answered satisfactorily at this time. Then, when all is considered settled, suitable appreciation should be conveyed to the leader with the assurance of unconditional support and back up.

One other solution, which can be most effective in the right circumstances, is to consider having co-chairs. Of course, these two people have to be compatible and accept their respective positions of equal authority. But they need not be the same personality type or even share the same ideals. One can be a figurehead and the other the real worker. This method can become somewhat like a business with a silent partner. Both need each other but perform different roles. For example, one co chair might be an extremely busy senior member of the medical profession whose schedule does not allow him or her to attend regular meetings or actively solicit on the street. But their name on a letterhead and influence in the hospital and within their peer community may well be very influential and effective in winning over a large group of professionals who otherwise may be hard to contact or not have the time to become persuaded towards the cause. In other cases, one co chair may be a man and the other one a woman, both of whom have fine reputations but function in different circles. This broadens the scope of the effort and helps balance the overall approach.

Now, having reached the stage of acceptance and readiness to take on the job, the astute fundraising leader(s) may want to know what obstacles or problems have been encountered thus far. Have any factions surfaced as opposition and why? How can the project need best be reconciled? In all of these situations nothing should be hidden. Any down side must be brought to light. All questions must be answered in a non-defensive way with total honesty. Nothing that could become an issue later on should be withheld. This is because the head of fundraising inevitably becomes very visible. The general public, as well as the media, will view this person as a figurehead and someone who is thought of as the main spokesperson for the project. He/she will be expected to reply instantaneously to the voices of doubt or to criticism levied by those who are against the idea. In short, he or she has to maintain a high level of momentum and be seen as a leader who is driven to achieve the main goal, in spite of the many little setbacks along the way. Experience and understanding lets most of us know that nothing in this life is perfect. There will always be factors, which, in retrospect, could have been improved upon. But 5% of error should not allow 95% of good stuff to be thrown away or abandoned.

The team

Occasionally, a fundraising leader will decide that he/she can manage by themselves without the hassle of convening meetings and becoming responsible for other people's actions or inactions. For example, lets say that $1000 needs to be raised to sponsor or underwrite a special event or for a sudden urgent community need. The leader might attend one short meeting or even call on the phone with the message: "Just leave it to me." A few minutes later he/she may allocate thirty minutes of their time and make ten telephone calls to peers, business leaders and a couple of retired individuals, asking each of them for a quick $100. The explanation for the request will be short and to the point and in reality, an eleventh party may be contacted to produce an extra $100 so that an appropriate thank you can appear in the paper the following week and letters of thanks signed and mailed within a few days. This type of result is clear. The objective has been accomplished. The time involved has been minimal and other people's time and talents have been put on hold or reserved for a bigger or more important project.

More normally, however, the board and the fundraising leader should work together to produce a capable and hard working group of people who are dedicated to the cause and willing to give of their time. Early on, a pep rally atmosphere should prevail. Genuine thanks should be conveyed to all participants. The main plan should be outlined and sold. Then the leader should define his/her strategy and timings. Responsibilities need to be allocated and there must be accountability. The actual number of people involved will depend on the size of the goal. Sometimes two or three are sufficient. Other times, it may require twenty. But in all cases, it is wise to elicit the various skills and interests of those present. Some may be great at word processing and office administration. Others may want to have input for a letter writing campaign and others will be happy to stuff envelopes, produce data bases, do bookkeeping, perform deliveries, help with support material and follow up, man telephones or simply run errands. There is also a need for a suitable and really competent person to become the PR or media liaison. And in the case of an event, there will be tasks like booking of the facility, coordination, catering, decorations, seating plans, place cards, flowers and entertainment. All of these tasks are necessary but the tail should not be allowed to wag the dog. What we really need are people who are willing and posses the characteristics required to get out there and meet potential donors at their places of work or even at their homes. Sometimes, this involves setting up a lunch date or catching them at a social function or club meeting. And for special events, marketing of tickets is undoubtedly the most important task of all.

All members of the team of fundraisers need to work together and cohesively. Everyone needs to be instilled with a feeling of pride. Regular meetings need to be set to monitor progress, bring everybody up to date, share successes and push towards the accomplishment of the goal.

Morale is so important and the effort should not be allowed to sag, especially at the time when most people are exhausted and steam seems to be running out. Perhaps a little reward may become necessary to rejuvenate the effort and generate a final burst of enthusiasm, prior to a victory celebration. This can be in the form of incentives for individuals and/or teams, to produce the best results. The winner(s) get a small prize like a meal out or a bottle of wine. This is when appreciation is most necessary and recognition given to all workers. It is often a real test of leadership, but no campaign can afford to fail at this point, even though things might appear to have ground to a stop.

The Art of Solicitation

To be afraid to ask is to agree that failure is acceptable.

These next paragraphs are probably the most difficult to grasp and put into effect. Stating it simply and most obviously, the best fundraisers are the leaders and/or the most influential people in the community. Not all are the most wealthy but many are. There are good reasons that support this view:

1. They are recognizable and credible.
2. They are used to dealing with decision makers at the top level.
3. They interact socially.
4. They can often solicit a donation or item on the phone, to a peer, in a minute or so.
5. They have a track record of success.
6. They are leaders and can focus in to the subject very quickly.
7. They have lots of confidence and, in some cases, leverage.

The ideal fundraising leader

Here are some of the characteristics that serve well for a chair of a fundraising committee:

- Very well known and respected in the community.

- Able to deal one on one with bank presidents.
- Known to city and county officers and staff.
- Previous experience with many fundraisers.
- A good giver him/herself.
- Good at public speaking and able to present well.
- Hard working.
- Good organizer.
- Good with media including knowledge of how they function.
- Passion for the project.
- Able to motivate others.
- A "promoter" (in the right sense of the word).
- Able to set realistic goals and achieve them.
- Understand accountability and hold others accountable.
- Endurance and follow through, including the ability to hold weekly meetings and monitor progress and re-allocate resources.
- Enthusiastic and able to enthuse others, positively and by example.
- Ability to create a bandwagon effect.
- Really knows how to thank people and give appropriate recognition.
- Be willing to be a spokesman and handle naysayers.
- Oversee written correspondence, appeal letters and final wrap-up of campaign including plaques, personal letters and public acknowledgements.

Of course, it is no good identifying the perfect choice if that person is not interested in the project or is at a point in their life where the availability of time is not possible. In fact, most suitable candidates are already extremely busy. They probably do not need one more community assignment to augment their ego or to fill up their precious little spare time. But in spite of this, it is from these ranks that most fundraising stars are recruited. If the question "how" comes to mind, the answer is usually the means of approach. A major commitment requires a major effort on the part of the organization to set up a lunch or appropriate meeting with the person they wish to enlist. This function should have at least two or more officers of the organization present and someone who is a well-respected friend or peer of the potential candidate. The nature of the project and the benefits to the community should be presented and the backing of the board should be unequivocal. There should also be a number of previously solicited good people identified as committee members. In addition, clerical facilities should be made available and board policy discussed. In fact, the board should be prepared to grant considerable autonomy to the fundraising chair and accord him/her their full backing. This is done, in the first instance, by themselves showing what they have contributed personally. And lastly, if the board themselves are not fired up and convey this enthusiasm and passion to the prospective fundraising leader, the result will likely be one of disappointment.

If you can, try to obtain a commitment there and then, even if it is tentative. If, as in some cases, the potential chair needs to consult with a spouse or other party, start to lobby that party in whatever way you consider to be most effective. Nowadays, it is difficult for many good leaders to take on a public responsibility without the support of their loved ones. Be sensitive to this.

First things first

Good fundraising leaders all started out at the bottom. Chances are they volunteered or were conscripted to undertake a task force commitment. This may have been something like being a captain for a Boy Scout drive or visiting businesses in two or three blocks down town to solicit money for Christmas decorations or taking posters to various locations. They probably belonged to the chamber of commerce or a service club or other business or community organization or perhaps they helped out with a church stewardship campaign. What all of them had in common is the fact that they were willing to contribute their time and talents for the benefit of others. Most of them worked under more experienced leaders and picked up some of the techniques and learned what it took to be effective. They probably also learned that before they asked anyone else for money or a donation, they got out their own wallet and set an example. That way, they could look anybody in the eye and know that their gesture of support would give them moral and advantageous high ground.

After these humble beginnings, their experience and helpful attitude would make them candidates for committee membership and assumption of greater responsibilities. More practice could be gained by moving to the next level. More sophisticated techniques could be employed as confidence and experience widened. They would, by now, be known for their community work and results and often, this fact would be reciprocated back to them in business or in-kind or community acceptance. They began to feel good about what they were doing and believed in giving back, to the extent of their growing ability. Then, after two or three more fundraisers for different causes, they were ready to assume leadership of a fundraising committee which sought to accomplish a small to mid size goal (perhaps $20,000). From this experience, would come the time to chair or co chair a major fundraiser, probably coinciding with another promotion at work or the firm establishment of their business as a leader in its field. They would know, by this time, how to set goals, organize, and plan a major campaign and garner the support and loyalty of those under them.

Some of the things they would have learned would include the following:

- Absolute belief in the cause.
- Positive approach and overcoming of all negatives.
- Knowing how to ask good questions.
- Understand the organization's mission statement and vision.
- Stirring up of passion and motivation.
- Ability to get excited and tell the right story.
- Knowing how to touch hearts.
- Able to convince others and convey the fact that it cannot be achieved alone.
- Knowing how to "read" the board and get their unqualified backing.

Techniques for success

From the perspective of the busy fundraising leader, there are several reasons to continue doing this work. One of them is satisfaction and the knowledge that their acquired expertise should be put to good use. Another is that most good people who have risen to the top in a small community are genuinely grateful to that community. They may not discount their own hard work but they realize that this is their community and any success that they have gained is directly attributed to the local people who live in that community. Thirdly, they recognize that service to their community is a necessary aspect and responsibility of being a leader. It therefore becomes an acceptable and agreeable task that is assumed with pride and understandable obligation.

Nearly all significant giving decisions are made at the top level. However, ten contributions of $25 each are just as good as one of $250. I say this because many professional offices including doctors and dentists offices are hard to penetrate unless the request comes via a letter or through a peer. What may not be generally known, however, is that many such professionals give authority to their office manager to write out a check for up to, say, $25 or so, to any legitimate charitable cause that benefits the local community. If you are of the opinion that such a professional can and/or should give more than $25, the best way to get it is to leave a clearly written personal request, with the "cause" literature, with the office manager, asking him/her to please put it on the doctor's desk. Your note should say who you are and have a contact telephone number and a date by which you need the funds. Ask the doctor to please consider a contribution and to leave the completed check or pledge with his/her front office for you to collect. If you have not heard anything after three or four days, call the front office and ask them to give the doctor a reminder. If necessary, repeat this action once more. This may seem a little tedious but perseverance of this type is often what is needed to get results. The good thing about it is that the size if the donation will normally make it the effort worthwhile.

At the general small business level, the owner/manager knows from experience that they will be inundated with requests for donations. (My own business used to average over a dozen a week!). They may well start out the year with a line item in their budget for donations and contributions. This is over and above any dues, business affiliation fees, chambers of commerce, local development councils, surrounding communities' business licenses, support at county fairs, donations in-kind, several annual memberships to local educational, wildlife or health related entities and other "expected" contributions. They try to be as helpful as they can but are, themselves, dependent on how their business is doing. They also realize that, in spite of trying to accommodate far more requests than they have funds available for, sooner or later a major project presents itself, which calls for a super human response. Sometimes the business owner is caught between his/her desire to sponsor a Boy Scout troop going on a trip and being seen to be supportive of a large drive for a library or community center. Inevitably, not all those who set out to get a donation will be successful. Human nature dictates that special interests may well prevail. We all have some of these and we tend to be bias in our giving rather than halving one contribution to be able to give equally to the other. This can actually create pressure on many businesses, which can even get criticized for not appearing to be supportive, when, in fact, they have been overly generous.

How do we best reach the decision makers? The answer is usually one of two methods: Letter or personal contact. Either way the approacher needs to be someone whose name, position and identity is known. This is why it is essential to recruit people who are in this category and why it proves difficult for more obscure, well-intended fundraiser volunteers to be more than moderately successful. However, bear in mind, again, that every good fundraiser started at the bottom of the ladder. They earned their way up that ladder and worked under leaders to gain the experience that made them visible and credible. Soon their names became associated with success. This is why it is important to continually recruit younger junior fundraisers to start out on that ladder.

The assumption (a legacy of the past), that it has to be a man who takes the lead, is false. Women are often more effective in this role and may well occupy leading positions within the community such as mayor, county commissioner, president of a service club or chamber of commerce in addition to heading successful businesses or assuming top professional positions. Another very effective group of people are the spouses of successful people. And by the way, I do not necessarily categorize successful people as being the richest or in the very highest positions. Often the successfully regarded person is the one who commands universal respect, is a giver him/herself and who genuinely desires to serve their respective communities and are known and supported for doing so.

What works when out soliciting

- Two people, working together, ideally a man and a woman.
- A phone call beforehand to set up a time with the person you want to see.
- Being prepared. Know what it is you are selling and be able to put it over in two or three minutes.
- Have supportive literature, fact sheet, brochure (if appropriate).
- Be able to give a contact person with telephone number and full details necessary for being able to send in a check.
- If an item is solicited, arrange details for pick up.
- Short, enthusiastic, presentation emphasizing the benefits to the community, time frame, who some of the other donors are and plans to achieve the goal.
- Knowing what to ask for and asking for it.
- Explaining how the donor will be recognized.
- Arranging a follow up, to obtain a decision or collect a check.

How to ask

The way in which we ask another person for something is critical to the outcome. Perhaps we know that person very well and can do it totally informally or by leading them up to a point where they, themselves, ask what it is we want. If that technique works, great! But usually, it is necessary to find a way to be direct, yet not off-putting. Below are a few examples that can be employed, in the right circumstances:

1. "Well, there it is. I am hoping I can count on you to support us. Would you like me to suggest a guideline figure or shall I leave that up to you?"
2. "I hope I have convinced you of the need and benefits. What level would you like to contribute? I would be happy to show you what some of the others have given if that helps."
3. "As you can see, this is more than just another plea for money. It is really important for our community as a whole and your participation is key to the overall success. How much can I put you down for?"
4. "Frankly, we've all made a significant commitment already, based, in large part, on our confidence that our local (businesses or other), will come through. Will you do this for us? Here are the levels of recognition that we've come up with. As you can see, this amount would be appropriate and very much appreciated."
5. "I know how supportive you have been in the past. If we all do our bit, the goal will not be that difficult. How about $-----?"
6. "I don't think you want to be left out of this one! Can you give us a check now so that we can use your (business or other), as an example for others?"
7. "You could really help us out even further by giving me a pledge or check right now. We want to wrap this up quickly and be able to get on with the job. I'm hoping you can manage $----."

Understanding the perspective of the small business Donor

Even under the most dismal of circumstances, most small business owners will see themselves as a vital part of the community and will wish to help, to the greatest extent of their capability. This fulfils their sense of belonging and provides opportunities to thank the community that supports them.

Any notion on the part of people asking for money that the local main street (and any other small business for that matter), has extra funds just sitting there to hand out, is totally unrealistic. It has to be understood that many of these businesses, even the more visible ones, don't always show a net profit and lots of them actually lose money. When actual profit manifests itself, it is likely to be seasonal. This is especially so with the hotel/motel industry, the ag community and related businesses, gift shops, nurseries and construction. Many well-respected businesses may not break even until October. You have only to see the empty store locations in any downtown location or count the number of small business failures and turn-overs to come to the conclusion that "making it" is not so easy as it seems. In fact, for new businesses coming in or starting out, the chances of still being there in three years are very small.

Taking into account that before you even step inside a small local business, they will have been asked, if not expected, to contribute to their chamber of commerce, national federation of independent business, economic development organization, surrounding communities, chambers or business associations, schools, professional and other business or trade associations, and subscriptions to their journals and donations to various kids organizations. In addition, they will be open prey for churches, repertory groups, county fairs (for prizes or bidding) and a myriad of appeals that their staff or the staff's children are involved with.

Most businesses do see their involvement as necessary to maintain a good image and fulfill their civic responsibility to the community. This will extend to tourism promotion and other costs associated in helping to keep the overall community healthy and attract new business and people. Growth in terms of expenses always increases, but commensurate sales necessary to generate additional profits to support those expenses, is a much harder nut to crack. To make it worse, when things are down, most businesses are forced to lower prices in order to keep selling. This obviously results in lower net returns. And it is from these very net returns that the business owner has to figure ways to replace old equipment and reward his/her employees. In all cases, not much is left over to give out. But this is the scenario that each business faces before any solicitor of funds enters his/her place of business for a cash donation, in-kind item of merchandise, or major contribution.

Even timing is a factor. It might have been a bad day. Things might have gone wrong. There may have been some minor disaster, a vehicle accident, a key employee leaving, a need to redo a job or the news that a major account receivable has had to be written off.

The small business owner may be wrestling with his/her own cash flow predicament and wondering how they are going to meet the next payroll, insurance premium, workman's compensation payment, city sales tax, FICA, federal and state unemployment or state tax payments, staff benefits or a growing accounts payable and debt service to the bank. All of this may appear pretty grim but most small business owners will know exactly what I am talking about. Their expected role is to maintain a smile and not complain. In fact, they may have recently shelled out a disproportionately high contribution for another worthy cause and be considering having to cancel or postpone their own vacation. This desperately needed break may have been planned for some time in order to recover from a long spell of 60-hour working weeks. And if that is not enough, that same owner may be giving of their time in both a business and personal capacity, serving on several boards and committees, performing community service.

The main point here is not to prevent anyone from going in to ask for money so much as to realize and be sympathetic to the fact that the owner's temperament and time for you may well be impacted by some of these other factors. If this is appreciated, it will go a long way in helping to formulate an approach, which might go something like this:
"We realize that you are very busy and inundated with requests for donations but hope that you can spare a few minutes to let us explain something which, we feel, will benefit a large cross section of our community; one which you may feel a close affinity with and consider supporting."

Another factor is time. Obviously this goes both ways because you, as a fundraiser, will consider your own time valuable. But to the small business owner, time itself is money. And again, we encounter the various personality types. For instance, there are many fine business people, professionals or other decision-making leaders who may appear abrupt. They may have quick minds and be used to having to make decisions straight away. They may be sandwiching you in between a number of other deadlines. Don't be surprised if you perceive them to be saying to themselves: "OK, what do you want?, what is it for?, how much and when?" They are probably allocating 2 to 3 minutes for you to make the case and will be put off and become impatient if a long drawn out presentation proceeds at a slow pace. In fact they may well become exasperated and just get up and say: "I'm sorry. I don't have time for this right now." So, for these people, learn to be dynamic, hit only the key points and ask or suggest an amount to give. Correctly done, you will probably walk out with a check.

For other personality types, it may require a more detailed explanation, and for the analytical person, there may be a need to leave a packet of information with them to digest later. This will require an aggressive follow up.

Although the above refers to local businesses, many other would-be donors have been in business themselves and understand the perspectives shown. Some will actually have to convey what you have presented to their superiors. It goes without saying that if you have not strongly convinced, for example, a bank president, of the importance of your cause, you can't expect him or her to do any better job in front of their board. What you can do, however, is to inquire what the next level of decision-making is, and either yourself, (or get others to), contact some of those board members and lobby them. In a small community, several of them will be known to your organization.

Conclusion

Timing, methods of approach, understanding of personality types and empathy for current business conditions and climate are all necessary to be really effective. Sometimes, choosing the right people to make a pitch to individual owners is a must. When going through lists of contacts, ask your solicitors who they feel comfortable with? Who do they want to approach and who do they not? Try and find a match. And remember, all businesses will be very experienced with asking techniques. After all, they get a lot of practice. If your organization's approach is not professional, to the point, and does not end with a strong request for money, it is likely to fail or fall short of expectations. This will not be the fault of the business. It will be because basic training in solicitation methods has been disregarded.

Tips include the need to be cheerful, polite, upbeat, motivated, well acquainted with what it is you are selling and, most important of all, knowing when to stop selling and ask for the order, in this case, a contribution. Don't leave the matter open and don't make the mistake of expressing any misgivings, negatives, or pessimism.

I will end with a story. Once I was helping with a major fundraiser. We decided that the larger general contractors in the area should all be visited personally. I took on a number of these and one day, I went to a construction site in one of the newer sub divisions. There I found the contractor but he was on a tall ladder doing some work on the fascia of a nice house. I told him what I was doing and asked if I could make my pitch then or come back. He told me to go ahead, which I did. He remained on the ladder and never once stopped his work. At the end of my three minute pitch, I told him, with some degree of confidence, that we had actually categorized all of our local contractors and subs and that he was in such and such a category and that we were suggesting that each of these generals consider giving $500. This was quite a high figure but he was a good and busy contractor. To my relief, he looked down and said: "Give me a minute to finish and I'll come down." This he did and walked to his pickup truck where he pulled out a small case. I could see that he had found a checkbook and that he was writing a check right then. Obviously, I was elated. He then walked back to the job site and, as he passed me, handed me a folded check, which he placed in my palm. I thanked him profusely and went back to my vehicle, by which time he was back up his tall ladder. As I turned on my ignition, I opened the check and found, to my utter delight, that it was made out for $1,000! I looked back at him and he shouted down the following words: "Kelvin, don't ever limit anyone's ability to give to a good project!" I have never forgotten his advice and I hope you won't either.

Putting on an Event

> Turning a dream into a reality is easy. It merely requires action, doing, asking and receiving. To obtain the last one, you have to do the first three.

For the smaller community, an event is likely to be something which brings in a speaker, entertainer, group or performing artist, who will do a show or performance for one night. This event could also involve a meal or catering of some type and the necessity to provide a bar, serving alcohol.

Typically the venue is a local community center, theater, church, school or, perhaps, a proper auditorium. Seating may be any number between 50 and 300 or so or even bigger.

Very occasionally the speaker, group or performer will agree to do a show for nothing but this is rare and usually only possible when the sponsoring organization or a key board member actually knows an individual who is passionately involved with that particular cause and agrees to do the event as a favor. Obviously, this possibility is worth pursuing. Sometimes, a well-known celebrity has a summer home nearby or even has close relatives who could pull some strings. But even if this is possible, they will probably still want traveling and other expenses.

In normal circumstances the first thing to do is to scribble out a rough budget to see if the idea is feasible. Here is an example of what I mean:

Costs

Performers fee	$1,000
Rent of facility	$400
Accommodation and food	$250
Travel	$500
Posters	$200
Advertising-all media	$1000
Printing, flowers, refreshments	$300
Program	$150
Bar set up, linens, tickets etc	$200
Total estimated costs.	**$4,000**

Income

(Hopefully), 250 people at $10	**$2500**

Result

A huge amount of effort and a $1500 loss! And remember, there will be lots of help needed to set up, provide rehearsal time, hold the hand of the performer, people to distribute posters, ushers, active PR and numerous other tasks. The performer him/herself will want to be paid at the end of the evening and quite possibly want a percentage up front. In winter, there may also be potential problems with airport delays or bad road conditions.

An interesting statistic within performing arts circles is that most actual performance ticket revenue seldom exceeds 33% of the total cost of staging the event. So here is a more realistic budget:

Costs

Performer/speaker fee	$250
Rent of facility	$150
Accommodation and food (with host family)	$0
Travel (combine with nearby community)	$200
Posters (paper only. DIY)	$30
Paid advertising	$300
Refreshments (DIY)	$0

Program (DIY)	$0
Contingency	$70
Total estimated costs	**$1000**

Income

150 people at $10	**$1500**

Result

Still quite a lot of effort but showing a net income of $500, which is worth it!

Things to think about

If the event is a "go", what entity is it that is putting it on? Sometimes the answer is to show your organization as the main header. But more often it is better to advertise the nature of the event as an attraction. This will hopefully draw more people than just those who naturally support the organization but which others may view as a narrow special interest. In other words, the object is to have a sell out and a really successful evening, with your organization being a by-product beneficiary. In this case, the name of the organization is down played but shown on the bottom of the poster, together with the cause that is being supported. E.g. "Any profits or proceeds will go towards the expansion of our local animal shelter." Or, perhaps something like: "Sponsored by ABC Organization in aid of our disabled children's Christmas Fund." Just remember that for promoting purposes, it should be the event itself that needs to be the draw. Once you have got the people to come, it is easy enough for a good spokesperson to make whatever pitch you want.

Is your organization a charitable or not-for-profit entity? We'll talk more that in the chapter about 501c(3) organizations later, but for now, just note that the rental fee for the facility, as well as paid advertising costs, and many other expenses are less if you can show that you are, indeed, such an organization. And remember, it is you who have to be pro active on this. Start by getting their regular cost schedules and then ask what discount they give for not-for-profits. This is often up to 30% less.

Assuming that you do wish to proceed with an event, the two most important things to do first and well ahead of time, are to book the facility and secure the performer/speaker, preferably for the same date! Here again, should it be spring, summer, fall or winter? What about ease of travel, school semesters, conflicting major events, holidays, week night or weekend, church nights (like Wednesday or Thursday), bingo or swing dancing nights and so on. Try to classify who your audience will be. Is there a better night for them? Can you draw from other neighboring communities? And what about timings? Is there sufficient time for people to get home from work, have something to eat and still get there? On Fridays and Saturdays, will they want more time so that they can dine out before coming? And in winter, should you have the event a little earlier so that people don't have to drive home too late?

Take children into account. Will you discourage a family of four with two children aged 8 and 10 from coming if you don't have half price for kids? If so, up to what age? What is a "student?" You need to define these sorts of things so that half of the community college doesn't expect a half price ticket. As an example of this, figure that if 33% of the paid tickets are at half price in a hall of 300, you would be cutting one third of your projected revenue by half!

Venues

Obviously, a good auditorium or theater with a stage and sloped seating is the best. It will also be the most expensive. The next place to go is a community center or other meeting room space that has audio/visual facilities, adequate seating, restrooms, foyer or large entrance space and a means to accommodate the number of people expected with appropriate parking and a location that is easy to find. You may want a kitchen or at least a facility that can provide refreshments, and tables for a silent auction. But here are some other ideas, which are worth considering, although many of the following factors will apply to all venues.

Churches

Churches can be good but, unfortunately, will probably cause many potential event goers to not attend. Connotations associated with many churches tend, in some cases, not to be positive and will put off some people who would otherwise attend an event elsewhere. Furthermore, the use of a church sanctuary, especially if there is a large cross behind the alter dais, will even be offensive to some. Lets face it, however tolerant and non judgmental we may think ourselves to be, can you imagine a staunch Baptist setting foot in a Methodist church or a Jew, atheist or Unitarian looking forward to attending an event in an Assembly of God church?!! There is also the problem of moving heavy furniture off of the dais, which then has to be transformed to a stage. Some churches do have an excellent multi purpose or fellowship room, which they rent out to the community for a variety of events. They may restrict the type of event but quite often they will be amenable and will see their offer of allowing their facility to be used, as a community outreach.

Some of the points to consider include; who will handle the lighting and sound and exactly how will tickets be sold? Normally, a church is not allowed to actually sell tickets and so the event would have to be promoted in such a way that attendees arrive with already purchased tickets. This means having ticket outlets clearly designated, and promoted in all advertising. An alternative, which can be surprisingly effective, is to advertise the event as "free." However, it is also necessary to include in poster advertising and all other promotion that a free-will contribution will be (gratefully) accepted to help defer expenses. It may be appropriate to actually state that "a donation of $5 or more will be accepted."

Another tip relating to this method is for the introducer or MC to welcome the people attending on behalf of the organization and, within the general introduction, say that this is a fund raising event. Then add that although it is being put on as "free", it is hoped that people would understand our desire to raise awareness and that our ABC organization wants to be able to meet our expenses and make a little profit for the cause and that therefore, we hope that everyone will get out their wallets and purses and be generous! For the best results, allow people to enter without paying anything and encourage them to "put a value on what they have enjoyed" and give appropriately on their way out. Remember that you must then have good people with smiling faces standing at all exits prior to the end of the event with baskets, and audibly asking for donations and thanking attendees for their support. It is interesting that although some people will give just the bare minimum based on the opportunity to have a cheap evening out, others will give much more and in some cases, that may well be a $20 bill or a check to support the cause. Always mention to whom checks should be made out to and exactly what any profits will go towards. Much depends on how the cause is presented at the event.

Schools

If the school has a good assembly room, gymnasium with a stage, or a proper hall and reasonable acoustics, this could be a reasonable way to go. Cafeterias are not the answer. There may even be a possibility of getting the facility free, especially if kids can be involved. Again, booking and arranging the details with the local School District or school itself is key. Good relations with the principal, office and custodial staff are essential. On the other hand, a school venue does not seem to lend itself so well to the staging of a fundraising event. Nevertheless, for certain events, it can work.

Check list for a special event

- Location. Book ahead. Is it large enough? Parking. Traffic control.
- Licensing. Will a special events or alcoholic beverage license have to be obtained? At what cost?
- The building. Tables, seating and chair layout. Restrooms.Traffic flow. Coats. Silent auction location. Kitchens.
- Inside. Means of reception. Registration. ID labels. Tables for organization's literature.
- The main room. Table layout. Spaces between tables. Stage. Audiovisual. Microphones. Theme decorations. MC. Auctioneer (flow of items, spotters, clerical), Servers. Flowers. Center pieces. Door prizes.
- Other. Program (who, what where, when, and time for potty breaks), Food (menu, wine, water), Entertainment (music), Invitations. Photographer. Dance floor area. Advance publicity. Media to cover. Accounting. Wrap up.

Sponsorship and Underwriting

This is the key to turning a loss into a profit. Lets take our example of a performer's fee of $1000. If you are lucky and can find a benefactor, business or individual who is passionate about your cause or about the performer/speaker and willing to underwrite the $1000, that is great. Sometimes this is possible and when it is, appropriate recognition must be given. Normally, however, it is a tall order. So another method should be considered. This is to split the $1000 into four segments and ask four businesses/individuals to come up with $250 each, or ten to come up with $100 each. Asking can be done by a letter, which explains who you are, why you are doing the fundraiser and how the community will benefit from it. The letter can also say that your organization has selected, for instance, one leading law firm, one leading accountancy firm, one leading medical professional, one leading specialty retailer, one leading auto sales business, one leading financial institution and one leading engineering firm. Thus they will be exclusively promoted and advertised in all posters, PSAs, program and live introduction. You should also promise them some complimentary tickets. In addition to the letter approach, an even better way is for all of the board members to seek out a business that they have recently done business with or know the owner well, and just plain ask for their support in the way of a sponsorship. This can be done at service club meetings, coffee shops, social functions or by going into their place of businesses and asking nicely. You do have to know the top guy but in a small community, this should not be too disconcerting. In all cases, give these businesses 2 or 3 posters to distribute and ask them to help publicize the event and get some of their own staff to go.

Underwriting can be achieved in several different ways. Say, for example, the cost of the posters is $200. Can you persuade a business or individual to underwrite that cost? Perhaps the printer will do it in exchange for suitable recognition. Similarly, if there is a program, can you sell a few ads that will cover all or part of the cost? For example, six business card size adds at $30 each and two half page adds at $60 each would generate $300. Can another party donate the flowers or underwrite the cost of refreshments? Similarly, could someone be found to help out with the costs of the facility?

As with all event organization, remember that the object is to make a profit and that profits come from what is left over after all expenses have been paid.

The Silent Auction

(See also under the chapter on The Annual Fundraiser)

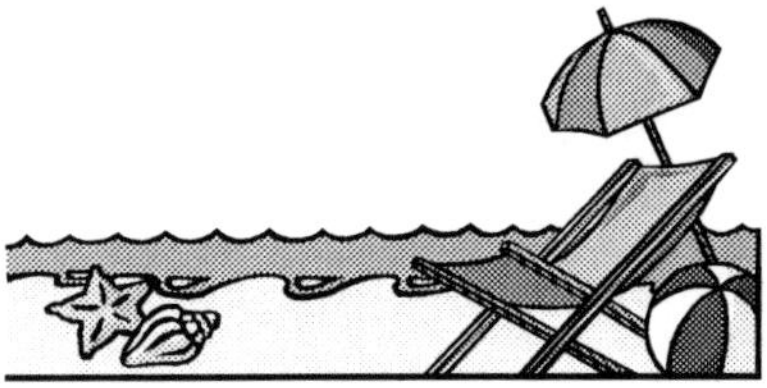

Presentation is what counts. A good item poorly displayed will fetch less than a mediocre one well displayed. Accessibility, good lighting, space and means of description are imperative.

A well-run silent auction for a normal event should raise anything between $500 and $3000 and sometimes, considerably more. There needs to be at least 20 attractive items and 3 or 4 of these should be good quality and have real value. Try to solicit practical items and obtain a wide variety of goods and services. Always get full details of donor, description, retail value and any special instructions.

For the silent auction itself, you will need a well-lighted display area with tables (and tablecloths), and easels if artwork is obtained. Each item should have an attractive bidding card, which should include the following information:

- Your organization name.
- Silent Auction heading.
- Description of item.
- Who donated it?
- Retail value.
- Minimum bid, if appropriate.
- Increments of bidding (like $5).
- Columns with headings of name of bidder
- Telephone number or address/contact and amount bid.

There should be space for at least 20 bids and spare continuation sheets available. Someone should be appointed to oversee the bidding and keep up with what is going on. The better the items are displayed, the better the result will be. This also applies to traffic patterns, ease of accessibility and opportunities for people to visit and revisit the auction area. This in itself means that the auction must be continuously promoted and enthusiasm generated for friendly rivalry in bidding. Try to announce a time for the last bid and devise a method for all items to be taken home by the winners, who have to pay on leaving. This takes some careful planning and an efficient person to coordinate.

Be careful about placing minimum bids on items. Try to get donors to give unconditionally. Problems can occur if, for example, an artist gives a painting that he/she values at $850 and says that the minimum bid should be $600. If you put this minimum $600 as the first bid, there may well be no other bids and the painting will have to be returned to the artist. Instead, put a small notice on the bid sheet that explains that the donor artist has requested that the painting's worth be acknowledged and that a reserve price is in place. Other possibilities include an agreement whereby the organization and the artist split 50:50 or the organization agrees to cover the cost of framing for the artist. Start the bidding at, say, $150 and let it gain momentum from there. Hopefully the final bid(s) will get to about $500 or so, at which time you can approach the last two highest bidders and explain that the reserve price is only a few dollars more and would they help us out by doing the little extra! It is a mistake for the organization itself to try to raise the bidding stakes by writing in fake bids. Remember, too, that it is always better to get $75 for a $600 item than to have to return it or not sell it because the organization bid $200 for it.

Lastly, all donors of auction items must be acknowledged and recognized. Often this is poorly done and discourages them from giving next time. This recognition can be accomplished by word of mouth, announcements at the event, printed in the program and afterwards, by letter. All time and effort in this department is worthwhile,

Benefactors, Table Sponsors, Artist Sponsors

Although this heading can also apply to general fundraising letters, some events lend themselves well to getting certain portions sponsored. For example, at a function such as a mystery dinner theater or fashion show, it is usually possible to get ten table sponsors. Lets say that these table sponsors (like a local bank or hospital or group practice or service club), pay $500 for a table which seats eight to ten people and the normal seat price is $30 a head, they can retain control of the table and invite their own guests or they can surrender the table back to the organization who then sell eight to ten tickets at $30 each to other individuals.

Similarly, flower arrangements and centerpieces for each table can be underwritten or even donated by florists. So can the decorations, table cards and even separate courses of a meal or wine. There is no end to the possibilities, providing there are workers willing to solicit. In the case of a golf tournament there are sponsor opportunities for holes, longest drives, teams, hole-in-one, putting contests, best woman's team, best men's team and lots of others. Once again, suitable forms of recognition are vital.

Advertising

This may seem to be obvious but many fundraising entities seem oblivious to the methods and principles involved. The first thing to really understand is that good advertising is imperative but that bad advertising is a total waste of money. Start by allocating an advertising budget, which should not be disproportionate to the total costs: 5% to 15% is OK in most circumstances depending on the number of seats or people attending.

Print media, consisting of the local newspaper(s), weeklies and other publications are, in most cases, the most effective. Flyers, posters and mailers are also effective if targeted correctly. It is better to put up 50 well appointed posters than to have 5000 printed and left in piles at supermarkets or not even distributed. A well-targeted mailer card to known prospects obtained from your own database is good value but newspaper inserts are rarely worth the comparatively high costs involved. In all of these cases the key is to create an appealing design and to do it as economically as possible. In the case of cards, fliers and posters, try to do them yourself on someone's computer, as opposed to having them done by a commercial printer. For the most well read newspaper, first go in and negotiate a non-profit rate and secure display ad space. If you can, ask for page 3 or page 5 or space on a page that covers special events. (Pages 3 and 5 are naturally the pages that your eyes turn to when opening the paper!) Newspaper ads are calculated in column inches. In many newspapers there are six columns to a page and each column is about 1.75 inches wide. A good size ad would be about 5.25 inches wide and 10 inches long. This is 3 columns wide and therefore 3 by 10 or 30 column inches. Smaller format newspapers will have different formulas but the principle is the same. Now lets say we want to place a 3 by 10 ad and the price is $240. Ask for the percentage off for non profit (say 20%), which would be $192 and then ask for the discounted rate for a second add (which should be another 25% off or $144). Now you have a total of $336 for the two ads. The next step is to say to the display ad salesperson or manager that you really want to do the advertising with their paper but your whole budget is only $300! Will they help your poor impoverished charitable organization? Result: A spending of $300 instead of $480. And it doesn't stop there. Tell them that because of their involvement you would like to put one of their reporters or entertainment person or feature writer in touch with your organization, to do a feature story, and that you want to be included in the paper's "happenings" or local event schedules or what's on. You could also give a good reporter a free ticket and ask them to cover the event. Incidentally, on the display add, ask to be called when ready, so that you can proof it and, with all advertising, don't forget these key ingredients:

- Nature of event, performer, speaker and topic
- Date, time and place
- Ticket or entry price or free with donation
- Ticket outlets
- Availability of tickets at door
- Sponsors and underwriters
- Name of your organization
- For what cause
- Theme

The other media consist primarily of radio and television. Think carefully about these. How many stations are there? What about cable and satellite? How diluted will be the reception probability for your potential attendees. What are the current spot rates? If, for instance, the rate is $20 a spot, $100 will only buy you 5 spots and the chances of someone listening to or watching that station at that moment in time is slight at best. Occasionally a TV station will have available spots during a popular show but these will be priced even higher and you will be competing with every other business. But suppose your event was to bring in a big band doing music of the 30s and 40s and the radio station was running a series of big band programs that had a good listening audiences, then that would be worth investigating.

PSAs. These are public service announcements that all media are obliged to carry free of charge. The secret is to find out what their criteria are and meet them. For instance, a TV station may want your PSA at least three weeks ahead of scheduling so that they can produce the spot. Here again, it is usually possible for you to help in the design by bringing in a good picture or sound recording and even agreeing to do the voice-over script yourself. This makes for a far better spot than just having a blue screen with three lines on it and no audio. Similarly, for radio, you could take in an audio clip or some other PR material that they could use and, again, offer to do the voice part yourself. If you do this, write a suitably dynamic script and practice reading it so that you can do it comfortably in 27 seconds.

In all cases, a good performer or speaker will probably have their own professionally produced PR package. Request this early and use it. There will be print-ready photos and bios and reviews that can all be utilized to promote the event.

Advertising is promotion. Think about other places and times where people meet and announcements can be made. Service clubs, church newsletters and bulletins (especially when an event is actually being held in “our church”), seniors centers, nursing homes (get info to the activity directors), chambers of commerce, city or town community calendars, other organization’s newsletters, traditional meeting places and community notice boards and even hotels and motels. And don’t forget that any event, which draws people into your community, is good for business.

Lastly, I would emphasize the value of getting a story printed or covered. Is your event newsworthy? How can its success benefit the community? Does the entertainer, performer, speaker have any local connection? If, for instance, it is a Mark Twain impersonator, is there any saying or quote that has a local connection? You get the idea!

The Annual Fundraiser

Even the most successful of annual fundraisers will start to lose its appeal in time. Therefore, the concept has to be continually re-vitalized or changed. Like any other aging process, youth eventually gives way to middle and old age. Before that happens a re-birth process needs to be envisioned and implemented.

The annual fundraiser can come in many different forms. Sometimes, a really major effort can only be sustained every two to three years but if a good formula can be found, there is much merit in standardizing the procedure and presenting it in such a way that it becomes a well-known community event that is both popular and expected. Examples such as; "The Altrusa Club Annual Wine and Cheese Party" or "Partners Annual TV Auction" become easy "sells" because everybody knows what will happen based on a good track record and successful history.

Each community will probably have developed its own types of proven events. However, even a potentially successful one that can generate a good return will only continue if the sponsoring agency or organization remains motivated and committed to spend the time in doing it. When such an organization decides to cease doing what has proved to be a good one, this is an excellent opportunity for another organization to pick it up and even build on the momentum to make it bigger and better. The next sections will cover some of the salient factors affecting the outcome of annual fundraising methods.

1. Annual Membership

Many organizations rely on an annual membership drive to raise a significant portion of their funds. A good membership drive requires the following:

- A database, which is continuously upgraded and allows new contacts to be added and irrelevant ones to be deleted.
- A designated time frame and calendar date for each "new year" to begin.
- A means of providing a suitable receipt.
- A justification letter or card stating the immediate past achievements and usage of monies from last year plus goals for the coming year and reasons for continuing support.
- A suitable space for members to fill in their current address, telephone number, and Email address.
- A selection of giving levels covering business, individual, family, and categories like benefactor, patron, gold, silver, etc.
- A note that clearly states what a member gets for becoming or renewing their membership. This may include something attractive for the higher levels.
- A space provided that allows members to indicate where their level of interest in the organization is. Give them choices like special events, clerical, tickets and posters and, of course, fundraising.

Advantages

- Probably the easiest way of collecting funds but the total amount will be limited.
- Can start out with a relatively small number of members and increase size and scope.
- A good way to publicize the cause and keep the organization active.

Disadvantages

- Can be limiting; i.e. if a business or individual commits to a membership, they normally feel that this is it for the year.
- Requires detailed record and bookkeeping.
- Requires considerable financial outlay. For instance, 750 letters, cards, return envelopes and postage may well cost between $500 and $800. That is about 30 memberships at $25 just to pay for the mailing.

Helpful Hints

- Look at the time of year for membership renewal. An in-between time like March or April may be better than January 1st.
- A return addressed envelope will likely produce a 10 % better return.
- A stamped addressed return envelope will likely produce a 20 % better return.
- A bulk rate mailing with an address label, although saving money, will cause some letters to be thrown into the trash before even being opened. To avoid this, at least have the name of the organization printed on the outer envelope so that the contents are somewhat identifiable.
- With so many organizations doing the same thing, at least try to make your membership card and letter attractive, appealing and different. Try using different fonts and colors with a catchy logo or fun symbol.
- Make a point to emphasize the need and make this request stand out.
- Look at current giving levels. Can the $15 level be raised to $20? Can a new category be created?
- The name is important. If you are starting out to build annual membership, names like Friends of… is always good and so are… Club, or… Guild, or… Foundation.

Recently, an organization that I was part of, re-did their annual membership literature and included a good letter showing goals, achievements and reasons for support. Also enclosed (together with a return envelope) was a professionally produced card designed to fit into the return envelope. The card listed future events and had space for membership levels and participation. I'm sure this would have been adequate but we went a little further. We approached the publisher of the local small town newspaper and asked him to show his support for what our organization was doing for the community, by giving us a significant break on advertising costs to put a whole page ad in both of his local publications. He agreed to do this and added his own line indicating his support. However, this was not just any old ad. We headlined it with large bold type saying;

"We're taking a bit of a gamble by doing this."

We then listed five points, as follows:

Reason: We, the OPAG board, want to be able to bring the highest quality Performing Arts to Ouray County.

But: We need support from our community and want to expand our Membership and become self-supporting.

Recently: We mailed out our year-end letter and membership card for 2003 to as many businesses and individuals as we had record of.

But: We know we didn't reach everybody, especially some of those who would like to help.

So: We hope this ad catches your attention – and that you will take a minute to fill in the form and return it to us with your check.

The idea was to catch a large number of people who we felt might be interested but who were not on our lists or (in this case), out of town summer residents. The result was very encouraging. We got many new memberships, some of whom volunteered to help, and the financial return was several times greater than our ad costs. The intention here was to make the ad really eye catching and to ask people for their support by showing them clearly what they could do to help and where to send their check.

2. Annual Traditional Method

This is more of an appeal that takes place without a public gathering. Hospice does a great job with their annual Lights of Life campaign. Cards and letters are sent out asking businesses and individuals to donate a sum of money in honor of someone else, for which they receive a token gift. The gift is usually small and in good taste. It may be an ornament for the Christmas tree or an attractive pin-on badge or broach. These sorts of income- producing techniques have a strong emotional appeal and can be highly successful because of the value one person may put on another, especially if deceased or coinciding with an anniversary or fond memory. Sometimes it is possible to tie in this type of thing to your own cause by stating that such and such a project or endeavor is in memory of someone who is, or was, well loved and who was known to be deeply committed to your cause.

3. The Non Event

This idea has become quite popular recently. It simply sets out to explain that while money is needed, most people's calendars are full and they don't want or need one more night out on an icy road with too much food and drink and the possibility of spending even more money on unnecessary items at a silent auction! Therefore, the non-event relieves them of this chore and in return, they can express their gratitude and relief, painlessly, by filling in a card and sending in their $25 or so.

This can be effective, especially if done with the right amount of tongue in cheek and with some humor and flair.

4. The Golf Tournament

The golf tournament is rapidly becoming one of the best and standard means of raising substantial funds. It does require a lot of work, and these days, because so many people are wanting to do it, the very first thing is to decide to do it and book the course, maybe a year ahead. If done right, a good fundraising tournament can raise anything from $5000 to $25,000 in one day. Of course, it is not so easy as it seems but here is an idea that definitely has an excellent chance of paying big dividends and, at the same time, provide fun and fellowship to many participators.

Like all fundraising events, the bottom line will be determined by the amount of underwriting and sponsorship. However, it seems to be slightly easier than some other events, to gain support from businesses, especially those whose decision-makers, play the game.

Hopefully, a fun event like this will grow in popularity and become a looked forward-to annual event that attracts many players and teams.

Here is an actual budget used in a local Hospice tournament in 2002. The final net proceeds were to $23,000.

INCOME		
FIXED		
120 Players @ $80.00	$9,600.00	
44 Hole Sponsors @ $250.	$11,000.00	
Event Sponsor	$6,000.00	
Wollert GMC (Shirts)	$2,373.75	
Underwriting	$1,125.00	
		$30,098.75
VARIABLE		
237 Mulligans @ $5.00	$1,185.00	
133 Par 3 Shots @ $10	$1,330.00	
Drawing	$255.00	
Auction	$1,250.00	
Shirt Sales.		
2 @ $17.50	$35.00	
2 @ $20.00	$40.00	
		$4,095.00
INCOME TOTAL		**$34,193.75**

<u>EXPENSES</u>		
120 Green Fees @ $50	$6,000.00	
136 Meals @ 9.38	$1,275.68	
Publicity	$600.00	
Mailings	$300.00	
Shirts	$2,103.25	
Supplies	$75.00	
$600 per flight x 3 Prize Money	$1,800.00	
Golf Carts	$40.00	
Shirt Sales 3 @ 17.25	$51.75	
EXPENSE TOTAL		**$12,245.68**
NET PROJECTED INCOME		**$21,948.07**

To achieve this excellent result, planning started in January for the actual tournament in June. The course was booked the year before. 300 letters were sent out in February to chamber members, new businesses, previous participants, the medical community and other contacts. The goal, here, was to get commitments for sponsorships and encourage people to reserve that date in their calendar. The emphasis was on hole sponsors first with the aim of getting at least 36 of these at $250 each. Next came the effort to obtain team sponsors at $320 each ($80 a player). Obviously, the event sponsor is the biggest challenge but a competition like this carries much prestige, and given the right approach, a major bank, community-minded company or other source will likely come through if the specific needs of the cause are sold properly. If this sponsorship looks like too much, don't forget that you can halve the burden by getting two businesses to co-sponsor. In the budget shown, the event sponsorship is shown as $6,000. Actually, this needs at least to cover the difference between the $80 per player tournament fee and the $50 per player green fee charged by the golf club. If 120 players take part, this difference is 120 X $30 or $3,600.

Things like golf ball sleeves, ball logos, shirts and the cost of the lunch, all need to be picked up by local businesses who can get some useful publicity and great goodwill. Prizes and auction items need to be solicited as well.

To help with other costs, the benefiting organization should become responsible for mailings, printing and posters (in house if possible), and, of course, the provision of several energetic volunteers to help. Knowing that this event can be one of the largest money raisers of the year, suitable importance should be attached to seeing that all possible support is given.

5. The Major Auction and/or Garage Sale

This event is a huge amount of work but can be highly successful if organized correctly. It requires three phases of planning:

A. The pre publicity. This is normally in the form of a letter to every business in town and all individuals on the address list. The media also need to be in on the plan at this stage. The letter and PR should announce the auction date, the name of the organization, the particular cause or project which will benefit as a result, and, of course, the contact person(s) with telephone number, Email address and other pertinent information.

To be effective, this type of auction needs to be touted as "The biggest auction of the century" or such phrase that will indicate it as special and not just another run of the mill unexciting event. The cause really needs to be accentuated, especially if it can be directed towards a strongly perceived community need. The thrust of the letter is two-fold:

- To sow the seed and get people interested in the event.
- To soften up would-be donors and businesses for items needed for auction.

To accommodate this, a strong effort has to be made to get donors to call in with their proposed items for the auction. This means having at least two reliable and good names to call and suitable storage and pick-up arrangements. In reality, a number of smaller holding places are required.

B. The cause itself and collation of items. The cause itself is paramount. Just to announce that it is for the Rotary Club or for The Hospital or Day Center will not be nearly so effective as saying that it is for the provision of an expanded animal shelter to avoid the putting down of 30 animals or to provide a new mobile mammography machine to serve the rural needs of the county, or a supervised meeting place for teens. It has to be something which many people can either identify with personally or see as a need for others less fortunate than themselves. Once again (and this applies to everything in this book), it cannot be overemphasized that something that touches the heart will always be the most effective. It needs to evoke an emotional response.

Having hopefully done this, the next most important thing is to collect, collate and organize the items. In other words, the main emphasis needs to be on getting items at this stage, because the promotion of the auction itself obviously depends on the quality and quantity of items pledged or actually in hand. And here it is critical to put out the message that because this is a high quality event, we want high quality items and not trashy ones. This means going door to door with businesses, making lots of phone calls, asking for a couple of minutes with Service Clubs, churches and other organizations like Seniors meetings and Chamber of Commerce and generally having everyone in your organization earmarking good items themselves and calling their friends. An inexpensive flier, distributed in supermarkets, athletic clubs and community notice boards, asking for quality items for "this wonderful cause", will not only produce results but also stimulate interest. So will a newspaper story. It may also be necessary to have a couple of carefully worded paid ads.

While all of this is going on, one or two of the Board or officers or organizers should be specifically soliciting half a dozen big ticket items like a good drivable second hand car, a mountain bike, a computer or vacation package, a few really good quality antiques or set of new furniture. These "flagship" items are the draw, both for the next stage of PR and also to encourage others to give and help create the bandwagon effect. For second-hand cars, there can be liability issues so be careful. The idea is that well prior to the actual auction event, a poster can be produced which announces the main event and which also can show an example of some of the really great items to be auctioned. In a sense, this list has to be optimistically demonstrated with phrases like "huge selection of household items, sporting items, antiques, furniture, exercise equipment etc", and "No reserve prices – Everything must go" and "All proceeds will go "towards---" and "Come!! Help support this worthwhile cause" and "Refreshments served."

It goes without saying that a good venue must be booked well beforehand and that arrangements be made to bring all the items in the day before to organize and, in the case of valuables, display a card showing a good description and value. It is also a good idea if each item or lot is given a number.

Who will the auctioneer be? Will he or she have their own "spotters" or will you have to provide? Can a local professional be persuaded to do the job for nothing? If not, can the fee be negotiated or is there anybody else who fancies themselves as an auctioneer who will do the job without pay? Either way, this person needs to be given appropriate credit. There will also be a need for clerks, a cashier and relevant paperwork. Even if you get a local auctioneer to provide free services, this does not necessarily mean that they will bring their whole team. Clarify this. Will you accept credit cards? What are the arrangements to get sold items out of the area? Will the facility be open the next day for this purpose and, if so, who will be there to supervise?

Other check list points include:

- Is there a sound system and microphone?

- Is there a stage already set up or will you have to arrange?
- Where will the refreshments be located and who is to provide? Can this job be delegated to another group as a concession in return for a percentage of the income?
- What happens to unsold items?
- Is there an MC or person in charge, who can direct the event? This person is **not** the auctioneer.

Another subject for consideration should be a garage sale space that operates separately from the auction. This is a matter of calculation and looking at the quality of the items. For instance, if it takes an average of 2 minutes or more to auction off one item, then no more than 25 to 30 items can be auctioned in one hour. If the auction starts at 10 am and ends at 3 pm, that only allows approximately 130 items that can be auctioned. Supposing the collections are better than expected and 250 items come in, it would be better to segregate half of them and put a really low prices on them so that they all go as part of the separate garage sale. For this plan, there will need to be a properly marked separate area, good signage and lots of help from the MC to get buyers to check it out. Perhaps, there can be a 10 minute gap created every hour or so during the auction to enable this to happen.

C. Final preparations and the Day Itself. Ideally, those people who are part of the organization should be easily identifiable with either some sort of uniform or apron or hat and a nametag with the organization's name. Apart from anything else, this is a great opportunity to publicize the cause.

On the day before, everything should be set out in an orderly fashion with plenty of space for inspection, and aisles between. Ask the auctioneer whether they will want to auction items on site or have them carried up to a stage. If the latter, you will need people to carry them up and take them off the other side to a holding pen area.

Machinery, appliances, computer or electrical equipment and anything else that is technical in nature should have specifications if possible or manufacturer's instructions. Items should be labeled "Good working order" or "Condition not known" etc.

Helpers should be allocated responsibilities beforehand. This means that leaders should be appointed to be in charge of specific areas, with a breakdown roughly as follows:

Event Chairperson and checklist

Allocate persons in charge of solicitation, collections, storage, categorizing and marking, event facility, security, treasurer, public relations and promotion, auction itself, including the tagging of sold items and follow up, clean up and thank yous.

It is always beneficial if donors of items can bring their own stuff and volunteer smaller holding spaces for the few weeks prior to the event. Depending on the value of items and the lock up procedure of the facility, there may be a definite need for security, especially for those who have bought and paid for an item but not yet picked it up.

Media support is vital. Ideally, some of this may be free in the form of stories, which precede the event, PSAs and interviews with enthusiastic organizers. But often, there will be a requirement for paid advertising. The print media needs to have a coordinated build up series of ads leading right up to the day before. Don't make the mistake of composing one good ad and having it run 6 times. Instead, modify it according to the momentum of the event. Change or add attractive items to be auctioned. Reemphasize the size and importance of the event. Negotiate with the paper(s) that your paid ad money deserves at least two good stories in return. Be prepared to have more than one angle to pitch. The goal should be to build to a strong climax the day before and create an air of expectancy about reaching the financial goal and making the cause or project happen.

Local radio may be able to do a live outside broadcast early on the day of the event. If so, have the most enthusiastic member of the organization really talk it up and literally ask people to come and support the event. Make it into a pep rally! "Everyone else is coming! See you there!!" Any peripheral things like refreshments, a band or group or entertainment for the kids are also recommended but not to the extent that it takes effort or energy away from the main objective.

Auction crowds are sometimes fickle. Everyone is coming to get a bargain. To most, the cause is secondary. That is why the MC and auctioneer have to constantly convey the message that everything bid on will help such and such and benefit the community. The really successful event will generate a spirit of empathy and goodwill.

The event chairperson will need to evaluate the mood, ebb and flow and be willing to manipulate the order and timings of items being brought up for auction. For instance, if a 1956 Ford Thunderbird is to be auctioned but is still standing there at 2.30 pm when 80% of the crowd has gone home, the result may well be less than expected. Sometimes, a group of bidders will actually ask for an item to be brought foreword because they have to leave soon. If so, accommodate them. In reality, this is more of a "feel" than anything else and requires sensitivity and quick action. In all cases, tight liaison between the event chair and the auctioneer is essential. This may entail the auctioneer being told that we need to go a little faster, or that certain lots must jump the queue or that several smaller lots be combined. Whatever happens, the idea is that everything is auctioned off while people are still there. This may involve the recruiting of more helpers to speed up the process because a slow moving auction loses its zest and the crowd lose interest. You cannot afford this to happen. Somehow, whatever it takes, the event must be kept alive, bubbly and entertaining.

D. Not to Forget. One of the incentives for giving is to get a receipt for tax purposes. Another reason, for some, is the recognition: To be seen giving back to the community. This is especially so for retailers who often see their generosity as deserving of some positive publicity, either by store name or brand name. In both of these cases the necessity exists to produce a form of acknowledgment receipt that includes the following:

Name of Organization.
Event description and Cause.
Name of Donor or Business.
Item Description.
Value.
Collected/Received by.... (Note: This info can be useful in case of a mishap)
Date....
Thank you.
Sold to..........
Dollar Amount
Date.......

When a card or form is produced for the above, it is a good idea to have it done in three parts. The top sheet stays with the item, the second sheet becomes the clerical record for the event and the third sheet acts as the receipt for the donor. Note however, that although this method is OK for the majority of items, it may also be necessary and prudent to acknowledge receipt for larger value items by formal letter. Having said this, a fourth copy can be very useful also. It can be torn off and given to the auctioneer so that he/she can see all the relevant details pertaining to the item. (If four copies are too much, use the third copy and then re-attach it to the item after the bidding).

In addition to all of this, donor's names should be announced by the auctioneer. Whenever possible, these names should also be displayed next to the donated items on advertising, posters and flyers. This not only pleases the donor but helps generate a positive peer pressure condition whereby no one wants to be left out. Obviously, this requires tremendous promotion. Always find out exactly how a donor wants his or her name or business to be acknowledged. How they want their name, title or business description is extremely important to them and this needs to be respected.

For tax purposes, most people want a receipt that will be IRS acceptable. Tax laws change regularly but generally speaking, any donated item over $500 in value should be corroborated with evidence to prove its worth. This may require a formal appraisal or a valuation by a legitimate business in that field. This should not become the responsibility of the receiving organization. However, it is always a good selling point to promote the fact that donated items can be beneficial to the giver, tax wise. But be cautious if, say, someone offers you a painting that they value at $8000. By all means accept it but carefully state that the value comes from the donor and not the organization. Occasionally, it may be advantageous to get an official appraisal in the case of a very valuable item so that this authenticated value can be honestly proclaimed.

Conclusion. An auction designed to net $10,000 will require about 12 people working long hours over a 4 to 6 week period with another 4 to 6 people on the evening before and the day itself. It will attract a lot of attention to the cause. But its overall financial success will depend on the costs involved like rent of facility, storage, paperwork, auctioneer and team, expenses of volunteers and paid advertising. All of this can easily amount to $2500 or so. The key to success is the number and quality of items solicited and solid promotion. One without the other will not work. Above all, get the word out that this is not another flea market and certainly not to be regarded as an opportunity for people to get rid of junk or clothing that should go to the Salvation Army. Instead, it needs to be touted as a social event put on by quality people selling quality items for a quality cause but offering unique buying opportunities and tremendous values. Politely turn down unsuitable items. Fifty good items are better than 150 unattractive attic legacies.

With plenty of advance warning, many people and businesses will stockpile items ahead of time. Also try small personal ads asking people who are moving or sorting out estates to consider donating items for the upcoming "charity" auction in return for itemized receipts of suitable value that can be used for tax purposes.

Thank everyone concerned!

6. The Sponsored Event

By this I mean an event that involves from one person to a thousand or more. There are two types. In the first type, an individual or group sets out to do something fairly ambitious like swim 500 laps or run a long distance or hike the Continental Divide or climb Everest. They do this on behalf of a cause they wish to support and get businesses and individuals to sponsor their effort at different levels or per mile or per every thousand feet climbed or such like. Depending on whether or not they take out for expenses, the monies raised profit the organization or cause. This can be a good idea but is entirely dependent on the individual, group or organization selling the sponsorships. The other drawback is that normally, this method relies on pledges beforehand, which have to be collected later.

The second type can be highly successful but usually takes several years of build up and normally requires a highly emotional sense of participation. An example that has achieved this in my own community is the Breast Cancer Awareness Group known as "Bosom Buddies." Each year they have a celebration and remembrance walk/run. The participants now number over a thousand. There are survivors, individual and family supporters, business staffs, and even people who come from far and wide to take part. Publicizing the event and cause is important and information pertaining to sign-up and registration has to be made available. This is done by word of mouth, announcements at other community functions and mailings to as many individuals and businesses as possible. The participation fee may be something like $25 with options to contribute more. Registration can therefore be achieved beforehand with checks sent in or on the day of the walk. Commemorative T-shirts are issued on the day and light refreshments are served. Ideally, all costs are underwritten in return for suitable acknowledgement.

The key elements in organizing an event like this are:

- Have a large venue like a community center or school to gather and have a proper start and finish point.
- Alert local law enforcement and seek their cooperation to assist with road crossings and traffic control.
- Have an efficient system for registration, receiving of money and distribution of T-shirts or other goodies.
- Have suitable space for promotional materials and access to them.
- Have a mic or sound system at the start point.
- Line up appropriate dignitaries, officials and survivors or beneficiaries to say a few words.

- Secure media coverage (live if possible).
- First aid and/or ambulance service.

In the above example, it is one particular cause doing an excellent job, which benefits that cause. Momentum builds over the years and community spirit is called upon to show support. People feel very good about doing something like this and much camaraderie is felt. Another way to do this is to combine the causes, tasks involved, and split the proceeds. For example, a Rotary Club may do a similar thing to benefit Partners.

The distances and sub categories of walk or run or levels of participation (like age), are factors that experience will tend to dictate. Mapping out a suitable circuit is obviously important and may dictate where the start and finish point is located. Don't forget that if a thousand people turn up, there has to be plenty of parking.

7. The Jail or Lock Up

The Muscular Dystrophy Association does a very good job using this method. The idea is that a good number of local business leaders, professionals and civic leaders are "apprehended" and have to spend time in a "jail" until such time as they are bailed out. Although serious in its aim, the nature of the operation is usually light hearted and done in an easy-going, fun type atmosphere. The following things are needed:

- A convenient well-known location to act as the jail. (Like the back room of a restaurant).
- Several phone lines and phones or cell phones.
- Four to six work stations.
- A good, welcoming, appreciative host or hostess with one or two assistants.
- Correct paperwork including receipts.
- Refreshments and coffee/juice.

- An established time frame like 9am to 3pm.
- Goals for bail. $500 is a reasonable amount.

The first thing, after securing the venue, is to solicit the would-be "criminals." Between 25 and 40 people is usually sufficient. Each should be professionally approached and have explained to them what the cause is, who their likely peers will be and what is expected of them. Assuming they agree, a time slot should be earmarked for all parties and they should be informed that an explanatory package will be mailed to them within the next few days. Obviously, the organizers will want to schedule the day so that all workstations are not overcrowded at any one time. This may take some juggling because the business and schedules of the "criminals" will dictate when they are able to come.

The package should include plenty of promotional material about the organization or their cause and give selling hints and reasons that will help those who are raising their bail money. Also included should be various gimmicky items like a wanted poster, picture of a jail cell or bars and some "poor me" lines which plead for people to help in freeing the prisoner from their bad time in jail. There is plenty of room to be creative here!

Another part of the package is a sheet of paper with rows and columns for name, address, telephone number and amount pledged or paid for by donors. Details regarding method of payment or credit card or "to be billed", etc will also be necessary. The idea here is that many "criminals" will have the opportunity, and will want to fulfill their obligation as far as possible, before actually coming to the lock up facility. For example, if the bail out fee is set at $500, some prisoners will hopefully be able to pre-sell ten pledges at $50 each or any other combination.

Whether achieved beforehand or at the "jail" does not matter. The objective is to motivate all the "criminals" to achieve their individual goals. Creating suitable friendly peer pressure helps, and so does the offering of incentives. For example, all who raise $500 may be given a gift voucher for a good dinner for two at a nice restaurant (with the restaurant asked to contribute $100 to the cause!). In addition, there should be a more substantial prize for the "criminal" who raises the most money or, perhaps, another good prize for raising $1000.

Part of this type of fundraiser is having a good time. Local media will probably be interested in covering it and simple instant photos showing the prisoner dressed in a prisoner's uniform standing holding a wooden ID number across his/her chest helps with the theme. Newspaper coverage of some type, emphasizing the cause and what the money raised will go toward, is important.

Administrative details

- For credit cards given by donors the info must include type of card, card number, expiration date, name printed on card and exact amount pledged. Note that sometimes this info will not be exactly the same as that of the donor or his/her business.
- Also on the form should be the name, telephone number and business of the "Criminal" or person doing the collecting.
- The tax status of the organization needs to be shown.
- Provide enough flyers and requests for bail-out amounts so that the collector can send out his/her own smaller packages. (I suggest at least 15 copies of everything).

- Ask "Prisoners" to post the flyer (with their picture on it) at their workplace and at other public notice boards.
- Thank the volunteer "criminals" for their selfless support and work. The ones who volunteer are usually the very best in the community and you might want to ask them again next year!
- Examples of some of the paperwork necessary, courtesy of the MDA, are shown at the end of this book.

8. The Fundraising Dinner

This event can be a great opportunity to gather a core team of previous benefactors and supporters with their spouses or guests for a high quality evening out. Obviously the party should include the board and those who have already made substantial financial commitments, but it is also a superb opportunity to have these people invite others who they think may be interested in the cause. Prices for the event will depend on many factors but for the smaller community, here is a possible scenario:

Income	
60 people at $45 a head	$2,700
Expenses	
Cost of meal at good restaurant, in private setting with wine	$1,200
Cost of invitations, flowers etc.	$200
Total expenses	$1,400
Net profit	**$1,300**

This type of opportunity may also lend itself to an award ceremony, honoring an individual or business. It also provides a platform for a board member, organizer or chairperson to update the audience and restate the organization's mission statement and goals for the future. Ideally it should also provide an opportunity for additional contributions to be placed in an envelope or, better still, invite all present to commit to a dollar figure right there. If done well, this sort of low key evening could net well over $2000 right there, with the potential of gaining much larger contributions by way of future bequests. Done well, it is usually hailed as a great success by all who attend.

The degree of formality is open to question. Some gentlemen in rural communities don't exactly like donning a tux but, on the other hand, if this form of dress is recommended (as optional), ladies will have the opportunity to wear long dresses or put on something that they rarely get to enjoy. The main goal is to make it a quality event (suggested by the classiness of the invitation) but not so exclusive as to frighten off some of those you want to attend.

9. Raffles

The small unofficial raffle, which takes place at numerous functions, is something that lots of not-for-profit or other organizations get away with on a regular basis. Raffle prizes, like door prizes, are solicited from local stores or other business-related entities and proceeds from the sale of raffle tickets go directly to the cause. Usually, rolls of inexpensive tickets, like those used in a movie theater, are used where the ticket purchaser keeps one half with a number on it and the other half goes into the container to be used for the drawing. Tickets are sold for cash with the option given for a discount for quantity. E.g. Tickets are $1 each or 6 for $5. No stubs have to be filled in. The drawing takes place towards the end of the function after someone has really pushed the last minute sales and everyone is happy. Nothing more need be said.

The larger raffle, however, is a more serious affair. If, for example, a new vehicle worth $30,000 is obtained from a dealer for $25,000 and tickets are sold for $50 each, then 500 tickets would need to be sold just to break even. Actually, it is more difficult than that because costs involved in printing, documentation and promotion could well amount to another $5,000, which means that 600 tickets would need to be sold to break even. But to make it all worthwhile, between 800 and 1000 tickets would really need to be sold in order to produce a net profit of $10,000 to $20,000. If tickets could be sold for $100 a piece, then 400 to 500 would have to be sold, but if tickets were only $10 each, then somewhere between 4000 and 5000 would need to be sold. In all cases, this is a relatively tall order and would require sophisticated organization like having several really good ticket outlets, provision to display the car down town or at a mall or county fair or other public event and people to man it to sell tickets to passers by. It would also take lots of powerful verbal and written promotion on a sustained and regular basis, for at least eight weeks, prior to the grand drawing.

There is also one more vitally important factor. **An official raffle license** must be obtained and certain rules adhered to. Some of these rules are not easy to comply with if your organization has not done this before or is not affiliated with someone who is already set up to do it

Even though some States may have slightly different regulations, the following will probably apply and require meeting of the criteria shown below, which can immediately rule out many potential applicants:

A. The written application

- Names, addresses and titles of officers of the organization.
- Number of active members in good standing.

- Details of incorporation or founding of organization.
- Copies of articles, bylaws, charter, rules and constitution of organization showing that the organization is at least 5 years old.
- Membership qualifications and purposes including dues paid.
- Documents showing organizational continuity over last 5 years.
- Bank or audit statements, corporate reports, tax returns, etc.
- Designation of the person (a qualified member of the organization), who will be responsible for all aspects of the raffle including the license stipulations.
- Nomination of a games manager who must be trained and certified by the Secretary of State's office before assuming any such duties. (This person must be a bona fide member of the applying organization and cannot be a salaried employee).
- Specific purpose to which all proceeds will go.
- Show ticket times and places that the raffle will be conducted and the same for drawings.
- Note: Any license received to conduct a raffle expires on December 31st of the year of issuance. There will also be a fee, and the appointed Games Manager (after being certified), will have to sign a written oath.

B. Rules and Regulations

For Colorado there is a 31-page document entitled "Constitutional Amendments, Laws, and Rules and Regulations covering the regulating conduct of Bingo and Raffle Games", issued by the Secretary of State's licensing and elections division. As at the end of December 2002, there was also a 14-page update document and further updates are issued on a regular basis.

For Colorado the contacts are as follows:
Secretary of State
1560 Broadway
Suite 200
Denver Colorado 80202
Telephone: 303 894 2200 or 303 860 6975 for getting forms faxed.
Web: **www.sos.state.co.us**
All relevant documents can be downloaded provided you have Adobe software.
For other states, try www.sos.state. (Abbreviation of own state).us
There is also another 3 page State document entitled "Planning a Raffle" and a 5 page document called "Quarterly Report" which has to be filled out every quarter and sent to the State even if there was no activity in that quarter. It is also possible to request a schedule of Games Manager Certification Training venues and times which are held throughout the Sate. These are fairly often. For Colorado, there is a separate web address at:
www.licensing@sos.state.co.us Their extension at the main telephone number is 6402.

C. The IRS

There is also another 32 page IRS document (publication 3079 (4-98), entitled "Gaming Publications for Tax-Exempt Organizations", which is really necessary. Usually the Secretary of State will have this document together with all the other ones. Essentially, what it says is that federal income tax (and probably State also in most cases), has to be paid on the amount of the winnings, either by the winning recipient on his/her annual return of withheld federal income tax (Form 945), or by the organization responsible for the raffle.

Examples

- A winning raffle prize is $10,000. The organization withholds 28% ($2,800), pays this amount in to the IRS on their own annual return, and pays the winner $7,200. Or the winner fails to provide the organizer with a taxpayer ID number and gets the full $10,000 but then has to pay backup withholding of 31% ($3,100) to the IRS on his/her own return.

- The raffle is for a new vehicle. In this case the fair market value of the vehicle has to be established regardless of what the organization paid for it. Lets say it is $25,000. Using the example above, the winner will end up getting the vehicle but paying either $7,000 (28%) or $7,750 (31%)

D. Final Comments

This section is not intended to serve as a watertight guide. My advice is to consult with an organization that has done a legal raffle before and also to involve a CPA for accounting purposes and a good attorney to decipher the rules and regulations, before proceeding. Also, really evaluate the chances of being successful financially. I have seen more than one endeavor, which has either resulted in a loss or break-even for the organizer, even after hundreds of hours of work. Regrettably, what you are likely to hear are comments like "Never again!" or "You must be joking!" That is why we don't tend to see that many **official** raffles.

10. The Silent Auction

There are many fundraising events where the difference between a loss, breakeven or profit is the proceeds from an associated silent auction. Remember, if a silent auction is planned to take place, it should be included in all of the advertising and event promotion with a phrase like "plus a really neat silent auction" or "Come bid on some killer items!"

The first thing is to obtain the items or services. The secret is to solicit like-minded people and businesses who you consider would have an interest in the cause. If there is a board or committee involved, all members should be asked to come up with at least two items themselves, either from their own resources or from soliciting. The items need to be varied, not all the same category. Sporty things, dinners for two, technical equipment, travel packages, artwork, pottery, jewelry, unique items, golf rounds, quilts, football, baseball, hockey or basketball tickets, therapy or massage certificates, ski passes, movie theater tickets, health foods, catering, a llama trek or outfitting or fishing guide service, medical or dental exams, are all good examples. And there are many more. Real values should not be less than $35 with some values up to as much as $500 or more. In the case of a gift voucher or package of any kind, be careful to obtain and state in writing what the expiration date is.

Space for display and attractive, easy to get to settings are most important. About 25 to 30 items is normally sufficient. You can probably figure on an average bid price of 60% to 80% of the shown value, although sometimes, a good item will go for more than its worth. One formula that is used for a major annual function, for calculating the ideal number of items to be solicited, is to divide the number of attendees by 4. Obviously, this will produce many more items than the 25 or so recommended for a small function but sometimes, the whole fundraiser can be centered around having 100 or more items and making more like $10,000. The criteria here rests upon the size, quality and past history of the organization doing it, as well as the number of people and enthusiasm needed to get this number of items and display space.

Putting a full "retail" value on each item or service is a good idea. People look at a dollar value as marked and then see if they can get it for less so that they can reconcile the purchase as a bargain, regardless of what they actually paid for it.

In all cases, a very clear notice and a series of equally clear announcements need to be made concerning the auction, its location and time of closing bids. During the main function, plenty of time and up to three bidding opportunities need to be allocated to allow people to get to the place where the items are displayed and bid or re-bid. The MC or announcer needs to strongly emphasize the cause and try to create a friendly competitive party spirit amongst the attendees, especially if commercial enterprises are present. A last announcement telling of the bid closing time and the fact that winners will be announced publicly during the evening will stimulate more interest and rivalry for recognition.

Adequate arrangements need to be made for pick-up of items and payment. The more monies that can be collected right then, at pick-up time, the better. Ability to accept credit cards will aid in this. Otherwise, full names and addresses for sending bills will be necessary. It may also be necessary for someone to be given the responsibility of looking after items that were not collected, if, for instance, a successful bidder left early.

Full or only partial success depends largely on having a good MC person and having an attractive eye-catching bid card. The selling points of good items need to be strongly promoted as well as the need to push items that have not received any bids. Once again, the message of the cause and request for support will do much to motivate bidders and provide them the satisfaction of doing something good for others.

The last and perhaps most important thing is to give credit to the donors. It is their generosity that enables your organization to cleanly make a couple of thousand dollars for your cause. The donors' names and businesses must be continually acknowledged throughout the event. If there is an event program, their names and donated items should be listed if possible. Afterwards, a well-worded letter or note to the donors will be much appreciated and pave the way for another donation next time. This is part of the principle of giving and receiving and helps create a spirit of goodwill within the community. And bear in mind, there is often a donor or two in the audience.

An example of a bid card is at the end of this book. The nicer the layout and use of colored graphics, the better the results will be.

11. The Salon

Although this idea may seem inappropriate to many organizations, I include it because of its tremendous success. The Ouray Performing Arts Guild recently had to come up with a money-raising concept to help eradicate a deficit left by a previous board. They decided to put on a number of "Salons." Even the name sounded attractive and the enthusiasm generated has made the work involved relatively easy. The idea starts with having to ask some gracious hosts and hostesses to kindly provide their home for the function. These are usually some of the nicer homes with lovely settings. The home needs to be able to sit about 35 to 40 people in the living room and provide space for performer(s) to perform. In most cases, this also requires a good piano. Next, a high-grade performer is asked to be the "program." This "program" can be a more formal concert-like affair or an informal performance done as pleasant background music with, perhaps, a short segment of attentive listening. A team of two or three volunteer chefs do the food and wine. This has consisted of a sit-down buffet style lunch or an English type tea, with scones, sandwiches and deserts.

Well-produced invitation cards are sent out to interested parties about three weeks before the event. These have details of the program, time, map, name of host and description of some of the features of the home, and an RSVP. A small amount of advertising can be done but usually, this does not become necessary. Sundays have proved to be the best day, with the start time of either 12.30 or 3 pm. The emphasis is on quality with nice table settings, silverware and china, and there seem to be plenty of people who are eager to attend. In fact, each of their Salons have been "sell-outs" within a few days of announcement.

Here is a typical budget:

Income: 35 people at $35 each	$1,225
Expenses: Performer(s)	$250
Food and wine	$200
Net Profit:	**$775**

This $775 can be further augmented if sponsorship is obtained. Suitable people to ask are attendees themselves and the builders and sub contractors of some of the homes involved. Say, for instance, that a $250 sponsor can be found, this would result in a profit of over $1,000.

If six of these Salons are put on in a year, that would produce over $6,000 in a friendly, social way that is truly appreciated by all attendees, as well as the performers and organizers.

One great factor in favor of this idea is that there is no shortage of performers who love performing, especially in a setting like this. It does not just have to be classical music. It can be folk, jazz, R&B, Blue Grass. or even dance, poetry or other forms of entertainment.

Can you adapt this concept for your organization?

12. Other Events

There are several types of turnkey events that can be useful to consider. These include traveling circuses or carnivals, speakers for film or travel series, or contracting with a vendor to sell fruit or other commodities out of season. All of these still require many hours and people who will help sell. Therefore a good committee is needed to act as the go-between and promote the event. Results can vary from poor to reasonable. If, for instance, your community has not had a young children-orientated circus for a few years, this could be a big pull, but not necessarily one that would be equally effective next year. One company doing this very well is Carson and Barnes.

In my own community, I have witnessed some really effective fundraising ideas that have done extremely well. One such idea is to team up with a well-known florist and offer to deliver flowers on Mothers day, Valentines or another busy flower day. A team of people is needed with their own transportation who meet up with the florist and deliver flowers to the recipients. This takes the burden of doing a huge amount of deliveries away from the busy florist who pays a suitable dollar value for each delivery. Given the right circumstance, a group of about eight volunteers could make between $500 and $1000 in one day. This is a fun and easy way of performing community work, being paid for it and being truly appreciated by both recipients and the florist.

Another event that has raised a surprising amount of money is a Christmas Tree and Wreath decorating event. This can be done in the lobby of a local bank. The plan here is for the organization to have each member or team decorate the items and get them set up in the facility, complete with appropriate lighting and the serving of punch and refreshments. All trees are either donated or sponsored by an individual or business. Perhaps the bank will underwrite the punch and refreshments. The objective is to put on a high quality, seasonal event that attracts a lot of people at virtually no cost. (There will be promotional expenses). For income, every visitor pays a $5 entry fee and all trees and wreaths are sold via silent auction. Suppose there could be 25 beautifully decorated trees selling for an average of $150 each and 25 wreathes selling for $100 each, this would probably net, after expenses, nearly $6000. This annual event put on by our local Altrusa Club to benefit their many good causes, raises something in the order of $15,000 each year. It usually takes place in the first week of December or the last week in November (depending when Thanksgiving is).

Be creative. Find out what has been successful with other nearby communities. Network. See if there are opportunities to combine an event with someone else and cut down on the costs of travel and boarding. Sometimes, a performer will charge $1000 for one night but only $1600 for two. That is a $200 saving for each community.

Suggestions like a fashion show or style event, mystery dinner theater, impersonator, art auction or musical group are all worth investigating. Try to survey your own supporters. What do they like? What type of event would they best like to support with their time and energy?

General tips

A lot of fundraising events require the production and distribution of posters and the selection of ticket outlets. The decision on the part of businesses to stick up a poster is a generous one. The right kind of thanks will go a long way in insuring that your poster is, in fact, hung up and, better still, given a good location. In the case of those businesses who agree to sell tickets, they should be offered at least two free tickets. It is also a good idea to produce a special poster which clearly states that "tickets are on sale here." At the function, these people should receive suitable recognition.

There are always people who are unable to contribute financially but help out with some of the more mundane tasks. This group of individuals is indispensable. Acknowledge them, praise them and make them feel how important they are to your organization. They may not seek recognition but if they ever feel that they are being taken advantage of, they will leave. Only then will you realize the extent of their value.

Nowadays, there are several companies who are set up to sell you items that they promise you "quick, easy, profitable" returns for your organization. Sometimes, given the right timing and volunteer support, it is possible to earn a relatively easy few hundred dollars or more. One such magazine that caters to this idea is called Fundraising Products and Ideas and is a subsidiary of Fundraising, Inc of PO Box 690, N143 W5775 Pioneer Road, Cedarburg, WI 53012. They can also be reached on the Internet at Info@fundraising.com

13. Memorials

This is a touchy subject but worth investigating. If someone you know has belonged to and supported an organization for many years and has expressed desire for it to flourish and prosper, it would not be out of place to suggest to his/her close surviving relatives that, perhaps, your particular organization could be named as a beneficiary for memorials. Obviously this subject is sensitive and time is of the essence because, to be effective, the memorial designations need to be included in the notices of death and obituaries.

Churches, Hospice, American Cancer, Heart and Lung Associations are often nominated but there is room also for a local cause that the deceased is known to have been involved in. After all, isn't this better in many ways than flowers, which will always be sufficient, but which, themselves, have no legacy? Just remember that the wording should be something like this: "Memorials can be sent to (name of organization), at (address), in honor or in memory of (deceased's name). And don't forget bequests. This latter suggestion is obviously best done while the person is still alive. Most people are afraid to bring up a subject like this, but if done tactfully, it can pay tremendous dividends.

14. Final Thoughts Concerning Annual Fundraising

Many ideas are well proven formulas. Others are new and innovative. All take a considerable amount of time, effort, energy, manpower and commitment. Don't underestimate this involvement. Sometimes, the first year's effort will yield meager results but pave the way for bigger and better things in subsequent years, Indeed, some of the most successful fundraisers are the result of establishing community awareness over several years or even decades. These become well-known, well-supported **annual events** that are easy to be supported, both by people attending and the comparative ease of soliciting items, sponsorship and underwriting.

Any group that wishes to take on an annual fundraiser must appoint a chairperson or co-chairs. These people have to motivate others, set a good example and let those below them in the helping chain know they are accountable and need to come through with their allotted tasks. These tasks, in turn, should have goals, detailed responsibilities and a means of reporting in, with progress or obstacles encountered. Everyone in the chain has to be strong. There can be no weak link.

Unfortunately, what happens in reality is what I term "the surf wave syndrome." In other words, one fundraiser is never enough. There have to be more and more until they are backed up and become an onerous burden, resulting in burnout for some of the best people and hardest workers. This often means that the paid Director of a particular organization has to spend more time on fundraising than on managing his/her staff and actually overseeing the very programs and objects of that organization's mission statement.

The only meaningful way out of this dilemma is a long-term solution. It is the establishing and slow process of building an endowment or foundation. Both involve professional expertise and there will be a need for cultivating a good relationship with a CPA and attorney who are familiar with these tasks. That is why it is always a good idea to consider getting these people on board early by asking sympathetic, qualified supporters to be on the board or serve in an advisory capacity. More on this in the chapters on 501(c)(3)s and grants. However, even this pro-active measure is not a panacea for relieving yourself of the need to fundraise. It will probably take many years before the income from an Endowment or Foundation at the local level can begin to provide more than a very small percentage of the annual financial needs that are budgeted for, by means of fundraising income. Therefore, view even this alternative as an investment in the future and not one that solves the problem for this year or next. But consider doing it anyway because the sooner someone gets it started, the sooner it will become a reality and start to grow. Consider an Endowment that has acquired $100,000. Given a reasonable year, this might be expected to return $6000 on an annual basis. In about seventeen years this Endowment would have given back to the organization more than the principal amount and still have the original $100,000. And if it continues to grow, perhaps a sizeable percentage of the fundraising budget will be derived from that source.

Letterheads and Logos

> The first impression is often the last impression. Image defines the personality and quality of the organization, and instills either credibility and trust or their opposite.

Most 501(c)(3) organizations do already have a letterhead. If this is not the case, or if the letterhead is several years old, it is a good idea to focus on this important aspect of image and projection. Logos, also, become necessary because they enhance the general appearance and provide a means of identification. A good logo is catchy, attractive, simple and appealing. It can symbolize the mission statement in an abstract way and convey a depth of meaning which touches the heart. It should be something that is easy to remember. Use of color, or a direct visual link with the name of the organization or what it does, is appropriate. Images such as sunsets, trees, children playing, the elderly holding hands, happiness, hearts or other innovative symbols are all good.

This logo should then be employed in everything; the letterhead, envelopes, accounting forms, signage, vehicles, baseball hats, brochures and all other places and opportunities. It thus becomes the binding force, immediately recognizable with the aims and goals of the organization and the services it supplies.

Letterhead

For even the small organization, especially if it has a need to raise funds, a letterhead is necessary. Often, two or three versions are required. The first and main one should become the standard for regular stationary. It should incorporate the logo and be professionally produced. Whether the address and telephone number is at the top or bottom of the page is not so important, although these days, the preference seems to be to put address(s) on the bottom. Don't forget to include web and Email addresses and, where a Post Office Box number is used, a physical address for delivery purposes and for people to find you. Another item on the letterhead that needs to be included is information concerning your tax-exempt status. In all cases, consider the weight and quality and color of the paper and how professional you want it to look. This becomes an image thing. Try to achieve a balance between going for really good quality and conveying the look of an established and successful organization without appearing to be too opulent or flashy.

The layout of the top of the page is very important, as is the style, color, type, size, degree of sophistication desired and overall balance and appearance. Often the logo is something that goes "through" the actual name, although it can be equally effective when placed to one side or just under the name. Another element that is recommendable is the use of a slogan. This is the short tag line that many well known companies use. "We bring good things to life" (GE); "The power of dreams" (Honda); "Always wonder" (National Geographic Channel). Think about creating a slogan that epitomizes your mission and use it accordingly, just under the organization's name. Lastly, keep the letterhead reasonably small in depth. It should be striking and smart but not occupy more than a couple of inches at the top of the page. The same goes for the bottom of the page. All regular correspondence will use this version but during the design phase, take into account the need to have it formatted in different sizes. For example, if the main letterhead is to be used vertical (portrait), can it be adapted for horizontal use (landscape)? Is a smaller note pad size useful? And what about business cards and envelopes?

Other versions become necessary when it is desirable to show the names of individuals (and, in some cases, sponsoring or underwriting companies). One example would be to include the name of the executive director or managing personality and/or the names of all of the current board members. The placement of this addition can go at the bottom of the page or, (recommended), as a vertical list on the left hand side of the page. One more example concerns a major one-time fundraiser. It is a good idea to produce a completely separate letterhead that incorporates the name, address, logo and slogan, but also includes a headline that describes the specific fundraiser, like "Ute Indian Museum Expansion Appeal." or "Bosom Buddies 2003 Annual Charity Walk and Run." This version should definitely have a column on the left hand side or page bottom, that lists the name of the fundraising chair(s), and all of the fundraising committee. For best results, it is advisable to have some highly recognizable and respected names on this list. This may involve some subtle diplomacy, like getting one or two of the most influential people in the community to agree to have their names printed as honorary chairpersons. Another group, like the presidents of some of the largest companies, mayor, a county commissioner or other elected officials, could be asked to be "advisory members." In reality, they don't have to do anything except lend their name. This can be a wonderful example of bi-partisan or diverse leadership and it may be surprising who you can get to lend a hand in this way. The objective, of course, is to add prestige to the undertaking and demonstrate that the object of the appeal is important to all the community from the top level downwards.

The board members names should also be on this letterhead. It is this version that is used for the fundraising appeal letters and related correspondence. Because these particular letters will be asking for money, there needs to be details regarding the 501(c)(3) and to whom checks should be written and where they should be sent.

Not to forget are the envelopes. These, too, should at least have the name, logo, address and slogan.

But, like going out to get money in the field, you still have to ask these people. Most will actually agree to have their names on the letterhead if approached correctly. Almost none of them will step forward themselves and volunteer their names if not asked. What have you got to lose?

The Major Capital Project

Nothing great can be achieved without a strong coalition of people and groups who, together, acknowledge the need and develop the pride and enthusiasm to see it come to fruition. That way, cooperation is guaranteed and credit is shared.

Generally speaking it has been my experience that a small community can only support a major capital project every three years or so, unless it is reacting to some form of natural or other type of disaster. Assuming it is not the latter, a great deal of research has to be completed before the major fundraiser gets under way. In the case of a new building project, it will be necessary to create a number of small committees to study the different factors. For the sake of this illustration, I will use as my "model", a new community center with combined senior center, performing arts auditorium and break out meeting rooms, kitchens and a large lobby area suitable for art and other displays.

In reality, a sizeable project like this will require the support of other entities beyond the ability of local business and citizens. In many cases this will be in the form of grants. Other solutions will include the possibility of securing money through a sales tax initiative or a mill levy. These latter possibilities, especially when they necessitate a placement on a ballot, and a subsequent vote of the people, will require delicate handling and a strong ability to convince the appropriate entity that the project is, indeed, worthy of that amount of support. Diplomacy, leadership, creativity and selling ability will be necessary to achieve this with a really broad set of minds who are able to think in terms of combining the project with a number of other initiatives that can be "sold" collectivity. I.e.: something for everybody.

Here are some of the areas to be addressed:

- Location, size of lot, access, convenience and parking
- Design (Don't forget storage. There is never enough!)
- Usage and users
- Size requirements (how many square feet?)
- Costs of building and site acquisition
- Operation and maintenance

Other important considerations are staffing requirements, how many people will be served and what exactly are the benefits to the community. Also to be taken into account are factors like partnerships involving other entities. In this case that would include senior organizations, the performing arts council or guild, service clubs, and others who would use the facility for meetings, and the chamber of commerce (for convention size) and possibly the school district, government agencies and wedding coordinators. And consider, strongly, the created value to the community as an attractive inventory item and draw for new residents and relocating businesses.

It is not possible here to convey all that there is to know about this subject because every situation is different. However, here are a few pointers that may be useful for the initial phase:

1. Select and utilize diversified committees that are truly representative of the whole community. Include professional expertise like an attorney, CPA and engineer.
2. Involve seniors and their expertise.
3. Select representatives from Afro American, Latino, Asian, Native American and other minority communities (and listen well to their input).

4. Spend quality time on designing a package that will help "sell" the project.
5. Even if the final design cannot be completed, go ahead with conceptual designs. If possible, have scale models built and produce provisional floor plans.
6. Be well prepared to make several presentations. These should not be thought of as "this is what we are going to do" so much as "we want you to see what we have in mind and are seeking your input."
7. Never allow the project to move forward if it is conceived of as a "good old boy" scheme which will only benefit the business community. Even if the project is the brainchild of one particular organization and specifically designed for that organization, it still needs to be shown that the real reason behind that plan is to help provide something worthwhile for the community as a whole.
8. Lobby city council, county commissioners and other leaders early on, before pushing ahead.

To elaborate on numbers 1 and 3 above, it is interesting to note that Latinos now outnumber Blacks in the US and that between them they represent 26% of the total population.

Getting agreement

Probably the most difficult things to overcome are the different parameters each affected party will attach importance to. For some, an auditorium will have to have a balcony and be able to seat a thousand people. For others the senior center has to be separate and not part of the main community center, and it has to have a maple dance floor, its own entrance, craft rooms, kitchen, be able to cater for 300 meals a day, and lots of other amenities. The hotel/motel industry may not be inclined to support the venture unless there is convention meeting space for 2000 people. The chamber and business community may want breakout rooms and facilities for three separate meetings at one time. Others will demand that the location is down town and not "out there in the country." Still others will not give a penny if the facility costs exceed a certain amount. The sad truth is that many deserving community needs of this kind, never get off the ground because so many selfish factions and independent egos are unwilling to compromise. To this I say, simply: Eighty percent of something is better than a hundred percent of nothing! There has to be a willingness to surrender some of our personal wishes so that the greater whole can be accomplished. In other words, a coalition has to take place, where all parties agree to work together to achieve something close to, but not totally meeting, all of their individual wishes or pet conditions. The fact that nothing is ideal should not prevent the best attempt to accommodate everybody's input, from taking place. All parties must be willing to come together and show support. Splinter factions can damage the project severely. These parties have to be placated and won over. This is often done by according recognition and showing them that some of the other points raised have, indeed, been incorporated. None of this is easy but it is all so important and it must be sorted out before the project gets started. It is mediation at the highest level and it deserves delicate but firm handling.

Now that it's a go

The next step is to officially launch the project. Several things need to happen, almost simultaneously so this phase should be carefully orchestrated:

- City, County and Chamber of Commerce all need to be seen to be behind the idea. This is important early on because of the need to create a positive impact on the community and because, sooner or later, the strong probability exists that you will be seeking some form of financial backing. Lets face it: If you think that your community has a maximum capability of raising $150,000 from businesses and individuals, and the project is going to cost $1 million, then it stands to reason that the balance will have to come from outside sources. These include grants and the involvement of your local municipalities. The best way to achieve the desired results is to find out when the council, commissioners, and chamber board are due to meet and get all of them to allocate your project as an important agenda item. Make sure that you ask the media to attend and be ready to propose that you are seeking a formal resolution of support. To help assist this move, it is essential that a strong show of support in numbers, turn up to add their comments and back the project. Be prepared to make a really impressive, professional presentation and include details relating to monies already raised and plans for the fundraiser itself. And remember, all officials are elected to represent the people in their constituency. Regardless of what they may think, they will find it difficult to appear overly negative if you have 50 people there in support and can announce that $50,000 has already been raised or pledged and over 300 more people have signed a letter of support! The icing on the cake is to find a dynamic and well-respected person to make the pitch and stress all of the benefits.

- Call a joint press conference. This is not only to inform all the local media and emphasize to them that nothing is hidden, but also to let them know that you want them to be the first to know what is planned. Then add something along the lines of: "We cannot do this without you guys. Please help us make this happen. We really need you all behind us and welcome any suggestions any of you have to help jump-start this joint project. We are hoping that you will all work together with us in this." And when I say, involve the media, I mean at the highest possible level. In the case of a newspaper, this is the publisher, and then the editor. For radio and TV, it is the owner or station manager. Ideally, in addition to the gaining of genuine support, try very hard to enlist one or two media leaders on the committees. The payback will be tremendous.

- Arrange a joint service club meeting with Rotary, Altrusa, Lions, Kiwanis, Elks, Toastmasters and any other active service club. Tout the meeting as the most important community announcement of the year and formally present the project in such a way that invites their full participation. In fact, be prepared to ask each club present to consider allocating a significant sum of money towards the project and emphasize again that this is for the whole community. No one takes an in-charge role: it is a joint community undertaking. Suggest that each club look at their budget for the next year and make a commitment commensurate with their ability, obligations and desire to serve their community. Encourage all of them to demonstrate the strongest form of leadership by committing future boards to follow through by pledging, say, $5000 a year for the next five years.

- Even better, is the idea of getting together with each club a couple of weeks prior to this meeting and pre-sell the concept and encourage them to make their announcement of their commitment on the day of the joint service meeting! Suggest a total goal for all service clubs to achieve and try to get a bit of friendly rivalry going. No one wants to be left out or be viewed as not supportive if the whole thing can be hyped up enough to create a high level of positive momentum. I'm sorry if all of this sounds a little theatrical but it is what it will take for the project to be launched successfully. What we are attempting to do here is to generate a community pride that involves everybody at some level, and elevates that community above those surrounding them.

At all meetings, the opportunity should be taken to "soften up the would-be donors." Let everybody know that this one-time most important community appeal is about to hit them.

The letter

The subject of letterhead and names is covered in another section. This will deal only with content. A good letter should be composed and go out without delay. If it is too late, momentum will be lost. This letter should explain what the project is, why it is needed, how much it will cost and when should it happen. One standard letter, sent to everybody, is not enough. Consider differently composed letters to different segments of the community. For instance, letters sent to financial institutions should have more emphasis on costs, debt service, O & M and methods of financing. Letters to the retail or real estate communities may stress the positive impact on the community and likely increase of people moving in, especially retired families if, say, a seniors center is involved. Professionals like engineers, accountants, lawyers and the medical community may want to see greater detail in design planning and usage. Other groups may like to read about the humanitarian aspects of the project and the space allocated for activities. Is there a youth component? How well is the subject of handicapped access addressed? Does the location turn off some of the people for whom it is intended? Is there additional space for future parking and expansion?

Don't fall into the trap of having ten people review the letter for political correctness, style, grammar and tone. If they all add or delete part of the content so that it can't offend anyone, and insert all of their own little pet wishes, the result will be a watered down version and a weak letter. The reason for the letter is to evoke a strong emotional response. It has to be forceful and catch the attention of the reader. It cannot be wishy washy and "gray." Instead, it must be powerful and end with an unequivocal request for money. It has to ask for support, based on strong reasoning and benefit to the community.

There might even be two approaches, based on time and urgency. One may be a complete package with every detail and the other may be a much shorter version with a one-page synopsis - snappy and punchy. Perhaps history and connections with the past can be valid selling points and in other situations, it may be advantageous to respond to the needs of a minority segment of the population. This last point is not necessarily linked to a racial or ethnic population but could equally apply to a cross section of society who shares the same need, like a dialysis center.

Accompanying the letter, or embedded in it, should be what is termed a "case statement." This is simply the opportunity to spell out why the project is important and why the need to support it exists. It is your argument in favor, backed by ample rationale. An additional document, which is often a strong seller, is a good fact sheet. This should be statistical, show summary facts and figures, be informational and easy to read. It should also directly support the content and theme of the letter.

In all cases, the paramount issue is the need. This has to be clearly and graphically shown and the solution justified. Of course, it will involve a serious financial commitment but this is where priorities come in. What is most important? How can this project be shown to be the single most needed thing at this time? Can we afford to delay any longer? What trends are there that show that this particular project is, or shortly will be, a most important and needed element for "our" community. If all of these questions can be answered in such a way that lead to the same unanimous approval and conclusion, the path ahead now depends on one more crucial question: "OK, but what can we do to help?" As you can see, the object is to turn a dream into the sort of reality that makes as many people as possible want to take credit for and see that it becomes successful. But this critical question by itself is not enough. It must be answered. The ways in which people can help have to be clearly shown; Where do they send their check? Who is it made out to? When do we need it by? Can offers of in-kind help be accepted? What are the levels of giving and what are the levels of recognition? Do make this last part easy for the donor. Consider a stamped addressed, return envelope. Perhaps a photo op for contributions of $250 or more or an invitation to the next main committee or board meeting would be advantageous.

Then, there has to be follow up. This is normally done by meeting one on one with as many individuals and businesses as possible. In several cases, it may involve making a presentation (which is tailored to the recipient, time permitted and personalities of those making it). Some of these presentations are more formal in nature, as in the case of boards where they will be an agenda item. In some cases, it will score points if a number of packages are delivered beforehand for board members to review prior to the meeting. It can even be intimated that the reason for doing this is because you would like to obtain a board commitment at the meeting and be there to answer any lingering questions.

Another really effective component, though not easy to pull off, is to ask the local newspaper (or the one with the largest circulation if there is more than one), to consider printing, say once a week, a list of donors in a special column entitled "-----appeal." As a general rule publishers/editors will be reluctant to do this as it creates a precedent for everyone else and pushes into the background, all the other worthwhile smaller efforts. But every now and again, they may be persuaded to do it for a "biggie" provided the project has overwhelming public support. In addition to this and/or as an alternative, they will probably agree to a weekly headlined update and actually designate a reporter to cover the project as an ongoing story. Whatever you can get will be beneficial. The main objective is to keep the progress of the project in the public eye and continually state the goal, benefits and amount received. Later on, the emphasis should change to what is required to complete the drive. For example, if 80% of the goal has been reached, the push should be for the remaining 20% with a headline like: "Four fifths there! Only 20% left to go!" Or "Project fundraiser on home stretch. Community asked to come forward to make our dream a reality!" Excellent cooperation with the reporter in question is vital. He/she needs to become part of the project and be infused with enthusiasm for what is happening. They need to be informed that their role is key to the outcome and that this can become a triumph for the community and an example of community spirit, involvement and pride.

Giving levels

It should be decided early on how donor recognition is handled. It may be that as a general rule, all donors of $250 or more get a picture taken, handing over their check and that this picture, with a suitable caption, is given to the newspaper for publication. Sometimes the newspaper will do this itself but they may also say that they will only do it for contributions of $500 or more. Find out about this and establish a good working relationship based on what they say they are willing to do. Having said this, our small troop of Girl Scouts who raise $29 may also be considered a valuable contributor and a great tool to encourage others to give. This type of publicity is equally important.

Giving levels should be organized in such a way as to encourage a donor to go to the next level. I.e. $1 to $25, $26 to $50, $51 to $100, $101 to $250 etc. There are also lots of name categories that can be used. Here are some examples:

Platinum	Patron	Diamond
Gold	Benefactor	Sapphire
Silver	Family	Ruby
Bronze	Individual	Emerald
Copper	Sponsor	Pearl
Iron	Angels	Amethyst

Other categories may include local or national geological or geographical features, historical figures, trees, or any creative or appropriate list of names that have a descending order of worth.

The very top categories may merit having a plaque or nicely framed certificate of appreciation. There should also be a space allocated in the entrance of the facility for a large, easily readable, metal or laminate plaque that lists all the categories and donors.

Finally, although it should go without saying, a personal thank you note should be sent to <u>every</u> person or business who has made a contribution. This note should not be a duplicated half page with an artificial signature. It should be designed well, be of good quality and signed personally by one of the senior people connected with the drive. Ideally, this should be the fundraising chair or, perhaps, the board president or director. Better still, it should include a sentence or two written in longhand and personal in nature. There is a good reason for this apparent extra expense and time. Apart from being classy and polite, it is a fact that many who have given once will give again. Lets suppose the project will need an extra $10,000 later on or is still short today by, say, $15,000. Going back to the ones who have already given will likely produce another infusion of cash. This is because they will already have a sizeable investment in the project and most will be willing to go a little more to insure that it comes to fruition. Don't be afraid to ask them.

Goal setting and looking from where the money will come from

We have said before that the goal must be realistic. Going for $5 million in a community of 18,000 people is not realistic unless a particular high-powered benefactor in your immediate area has made it known that he or she wants to see it happen. Unfortunately, everyone seems to think that so and so who is a billionaire and has a property a few miles away will automatically become the savior for every fundraiser in the county. The truth is that these people are very well protected and have mechanisms in place to avoid becoming involved with every little local endeavor. This does not mean that they do not give. It merely means that their giving is organized on a higher level and may preclude a public demonstration of that giving. Sometimes great gifts are received anonymously from these people and at other times, their generosity is shown in forms that we are not aware of. They may also have several homes in different parts of the country and pet charities that they support magnificently. So don't rely on these people for a quick $100,000 because the chances are fairly remote. Some of them, even if they are reached indirectly, will ask that any request for financial support be sent to their corporate headquarters in the form that they want to review. That review is seldom carried out by the person you are wanting to contact, just because of a local connection. In fact, it is more likely to be thrown in with hundreds of others received on a weekly basis!! But: As Dr Charles Sanders, former Chairman of Glaxo has said: "One of the greatest joys of making money is being able to give it away." This is so true. Some people will always have the capacity to give and you may be surprised to find that a portion of these will actually give more than you think they will. Others will want to help out but may need (and be waiting for), a nudge or some form of enticement. In these cases, the consideration of naming a room or other feature of the project after them, may well be all that is needed to extract a decision. Ideas like this should be envisioned when considering the various levels and categories. Occasionally, these categories may have to be re-visited when, for example, someone shows a serious interest, and negotiations commence, concerning the naming of a feature after him/her or their family or even someone else that they want to honor. In this particular instance, an experienced negotiator should be called in and a price agreed upon. This price could become far more than the original thought-of sum and result in a huge personal investment, which becomes a real legacy, based on the degree to which the donor becomes attached to the cause or community. On smaller levels, there are many novel ideas that can generate broader interest. These include "personal or family" bricks, tiles, items of furniture or fixtures, sections of a library, entrance sculpture or fireplace, and even kitchen equipment. Perhaps one group or service club could take on the funding of a particular room or larger feature. In all of these cases, don't forget the recognition plaque or means of public acknowledgement.

All fundraising projects must be presented optimistically. Upbeat approaches are vital. You cannot afford to be negative or pessimistic. However, the goal and methods of achieving it should equally not frighten off any would-be contributors. It is a good idea to research what other major fundraisers have taken place in the last few years and ascertain how successful they were. What is the largest fundraiser ever done in the community? Can the community surpass that figure? If, say, $275,000 was raised for a library, then $2 million for a community center is probably too much. Perhaps $400,000 is more doable. And still, a lot depends on the strength, commitment and enthusiasm of the board, as well as the personality, track record and input of the fundraising chair.

For our example, I am going to call our goal $300,000 and assume that most of the legwork has been done to convince the community that it is for a project that has a strong majority support.

Method 1

Split the $300,000 into units, something like the following:

1 unit at $25,000	$25,000
10 units at $10,000	$100,000
15 units at $5,000	$75,000
25 units at $1,000	$25,000
50 units at $500	$25,000
200 units at $100	$20,000
300 units at $50	$15,000
150 units at $25	$3,750
Special events	$11,250
	$300,000

Method 2

Split the $300,000 into entities, something like this:

City, county	$50,000
Hospital	$10,000
Utility companies (including phone)	$20,000
Banks and financial institutions	$30,000
Professionals	$40,000
Wholesale/manufacturing	$15,000
Retail	$45,000
Service clubs	$10,000
Individuals	$70,000
Special events	$10,000
	$300,000

In this last example, individuals can be a broad category. It should definitely include seniors' organizations, arts councils, board of realtors, chamber of commerce and all other groups comprised of individual members. And in all cases, don't forget that in-kind donations like concrete work, sub contractors, site development and painting can count as contributions. It may be possible for city/county to allocate some of their resources for things like roadwork, gravel and landscaping. Utilities, too, can probably be persuaded to help with power lines and connections. (Some of these may have to be arranged subtly because there are always some people out there who will be watching to see where their tax dollars etc are going!) Sadly, a large percentage of the local population falls into the category of what some people refer to as "in the shadows." They tend to be not so visible and non participative. This does not mean that they don't give or don't have the money. It is more likely that their lives, up to this point, have just not centered around the joining and close association with the community as a whole. They may be consumed with their work and even feel that the world in which they operate is either not deserving or all they can handle. I don't wish to appear judgmental here, but frequently this group may consist of government workers, teachers, professional employees of large companies, sub contractor artisans (who earn a lot of money) and staffs of medical institutions. Obviously, there are many exceptions but, in most cases, many of these people seldom come forward and are never asked. Try, therefore, to penetrate this wonderful source because I'm sure, at heart, that most of them are just as generous as everyone else.

And don't forget the influx of new residents and retirees. Sometimes their discretionary income is greater than those who are still working and there are many occasions when people need to create some tax savings. Again, the aim is to get out there, identify them, meet them and ask them.

Method 3

This is the multi year pledge. It may be good for some but not for others, but if the amounts sought are high, it serves to break it down into more sellable portions. Church building programs have used this method successfully for generations and, under the right circumstances, it is definitely one of the best ways to go.

Advantages

- Asking a business to commit $1,000 for three years is more likely to get a yes than asking them to give a one-time contribution of $3,000.
- This method can lead to a larger grand total.
- Givers can see the results of their giving during the giving cycle.
- Donors get full credit up from for the total amount of the pledge.
- By getting pledge totals, the effect tends to help jump-start the campaign and help create good momentum.

Disadvantages

- It produces a heavier burden on book keeping and accounting.
- Most people will have to be reminded in the second and subsequent years.
- Some will be reluctant to commit that long, especially in a volatile economy.
- There will be attrition. Some businesses may not be around two years later. Collections may be more like 90% of the total amount pledged.
- It may dilute the next series of fundraising efforts.
- In the case of boards, the question always comes up: "Is a subsequent board really responsible for

coming through on a commitment made by a previous board?"

Other methods

A fourth method, employed by some successful fundraisers, is to start by splitting the formal goal into thirds. The top ten or twelve donors give one third of the total; the next 100 or so give the next third and the rest give the remaining third.

I realize that the character of each community is different and so will be the support and cooperation of key personalities like city manager or county officials, and others. Therefore the categories and percentages can vary accordingly. The object is to develop a formula, which enables you to take a huge task and break it down into manageable segments. Note also, that the very nature of the project will dictate certain directions, because each project will attract a different set of supporters. For example, a new high school gymnasium, track or skateboard park will attract different people than an in-patient facility for Hospice or a new animal shelter.

Undoubtedly one of the most important issues centers around O&M (operations and maintenance). Who will staff the facility? Who will pick up the slack on maintenance costs? After it is built, who actually "owns" the facility? Is it private or public? What will be necessary to insure that it does not become a "white elephant"? Well, lets face reality. On the one hand, the facility is either going to be a privately funded building that can be financially self sufficient or an agency type building that conducts its own capital project fundraiser and then proceeds to operate by producing income from a combination of grants, government subsidies or reimbursements and continuous fundraising activities. On the other hand, my community center example comes to mind. This type of venture will never be able to pay for itself and no amount of fundraising will cover all the building costs. Instead, it really has to become the property of the community, represented by local government, who hopefully have the insight to see that such a useful addition to their community will eventually help to bring more people in, strengthen the inventory base and produce more sales tax. All of this leads to one conclusion. In the vast majority of cases, a project such as this cannot fly without city and/or county approval and support. They will need to find a way to fund a significant portion of the initial construction costs and budget O&M expenses. Some of these costs can be offset by income from use permits and other means but to think that a facility like this can break even, financially, or pay for itself, is pie in the sky!

While the above is obviously critical to the overall success, other associated smaller fundraisers like bake sales, garage sales, auctions, raffles and proceeds from smaller events all count and, in fact, broaden the base of the endeavor.

Momentum

The strategy should be to get a jump-start. If, for instance, in our example of $300,000, the city and county could each earmark $20,000 out of their general fund account, and the joint service clubs could come up with $10,000, and three major donors would commit $5,000 each, and the respective board/committee tangibly demonstrated their support by producing $2,500, we would have $67,500. Using this as leverage, we should be able to approach our local utility or someone like an earth moving contractor to each pitch in the equivalent of $10,000 in in-kind work. Now we have $87,500 or nearly 30% of the goal. Don't think this is far fetched. Instead, consider it as the type of thinking that stimulates results. In fact, leadership of this kind is virtually indispensable if the project is to receive the broad based support it will require and the backing of the community's most respected men and women, together with that of the businesses that they control. This is what leads to the bandwagon effect and the plain and simple peer pressure that gets most of the other businesses to participate.

Some other tips

The major fundraiser definitely requires a good deal of groundwork. To try and do it casually is a mistake. A systematic approach is important for success. For example, it is often assumed that the main street retail sector is the first, best and only source. All three perceptions are wrong. Main Street tends to be the hardest hit because they are the most visible, the easiest to find and are often owned by local business people who are well known and approachable. In reality, a lot of them are working horrendous hours trying to break even. They are always the hardest hit and their projected net profit, which is probably in the low single digits, just does not allow them to provide funds or in-kind donations to everybody. Nevertheless they make every effort to help, and the majority tries to do the best they can. They are just not always so well endowed as people think!

Instead, do some homework. Ask a few of your local CPAs and others in the community who are in the know; "Who is doing well?" Try to find out where some of the well healed, but more private people, hang out. Make sure their addresses and other means of contact are entered into databases. When are they in town? How can they best be approached? Often some of the local businesses will be dealing with them and can provide useful leads.

So often, a major portion of potential donors never even get contacted. Here is a list of some other sources. Depending on the type of community, there will be lots of others. Just make sure that all of them are covered. And remember the adage once more, the more you ask, the greater will be the result!

Mortgage companies and savings and loans
Insurance
Storage units
Home decorating
Liquor stores
Office supplies
Printing shops
Freight (like UPS, FedEx, common carriers)
Car rentals
Marine businesses
Funeral homes
Entertainment (cinemas, bowling alleys, night clubs etc)
Beauty shops including hairdressers, nails and tanning
Mobile home sales
Glass
Fast foods
Outfitters
Lumber companies
Irrigation and pipe
Travel agencies
Convenience stores
Propane gas
Excavation
Sign writers and signs
Auto including parts, service, sales, lube, tires, body shops
RV and snowmobile and skidoo sales
Cable
Realtors
Audio
Jewelers
Health clubs
Sporting goods
Restaurants
Hotels and motels
General contractors
Developers
Clothing stores
Coffee shops

Beverage distributors
Booksellers
Florists
Garden Centers
Health food stores
Appliance sales
Working ranch owners and the ag community
Telephone and cable or satellite companies
Natural gas and oil companies
Large plant operators
Computer related businesses
Bookkeeping services
Sub contractors

Naturally, all professionals like doctors, dentists, orthodontists, veterinarians, engineers, architects, lawyers, accountants, tax preparers and pharmacists need to be sub categorized and other not-so-visible businesses like artisans, consultants, therapists, coaches, appraisers, title companies, campgrounds, cellular phone guys and medical billing services should not be excluded. The above is by no means exhaustive but seeks only to stimulate you into looking at the potential. The point here is that there are literally hundreds of businesses out there and they all need to be contacted. Someone has to make a list and break it down for the actual askers to contact. If a good database exists, update it. If it does not, here are some sources:

- The Yellow Pages
- The Chamber of Commerce Membership Directory
- Contact Service clubs to see if they will share their membership lists
- Contact other organizations to see if they will do the same

- Find out if the local newspaper, city or chamber has a master list showing every community organization, including clubs
- See if other fundraising leaders will share their own lists

Now split all the names into the following categories. (There may be more).

- Civic – county, city, hospital, schools etc
- Service clubs and other well established organizations that help out in the community
- Businesses
- Individuals

Under businesses, sub-categorize under:

- Wholesale and manufacturing.
- Banks and financial institutions.
- Retail: Break down into geographical areas or into sub categories like home decorating and furniture, clothing, gifts and jewelry, auto etc.
- Professional: Further breakdown into engineers and architects, legal, accounting, medical doctors and dentists, etc.
- Utilities
- General contractors; Further breakdown into subs like plumbing, electrical, HVAC, drywall, roofing, framing, foundations, site work, landscaping, painting, etc.

Under Individuals: Breakdown into:

- heavy hitters
- known supporters
- seniors
- new residents, etc.

Timing

Timing is extremely important. There is nothing worse than three deserving entities unknowingly getting ready to launch their own fundraisers without realizing that the other two have chosen the same month to do theirs. Even if they are planned for six months apart, all of them will be severely diluted. In some ways this is unfortunate because the one that pre-publicizes their effort first and promotes it as the major fundraiser of the year will likely frighten off either one or both of the others. Unfortunately, such is life. With experience in this field, the fundraising chair will seek to make contact with and be open to the other major fundraising campaigns. Normally, in a small community, the news of something big coming down the line is not a secret. Sometimes (regrettably), there is a sort of jealousy, which can exist, which fosters a more closed atmosphere and lack of cooperation. More normally, the feeling of all being on the same side prevails and fundraising leaders or paid special events coordinators can get together and discuss future plans, designed to avoid unnecessary competition or, in the worst case, sabotage.

When the goal and time frame have been agreed, the fundraising leader, board and/or committee has to accept the challenge and be willing to prioritize their schedules to make it work. There can be no splitting of goals. The aim becomes one of total success for the project in hand. This means focusing very clearly on that subject and not undertaking other commitments, which will hinder the desired result.

The actual time of year is also a factor. Often, it will be dictated by other issues such as the stage of the proposed project or some other form of spontaneous or urgent need. However, although it may appear obvious, the following are **not** regarded as the best times to kick off a major fundraiser:

The months of December and January.
Times coinciding with political campaigns.
Summer vacation times.
Too soon after another large fundraiser.

Generally speaking, starting in spring is a good time and so is early fall. But don't be unduly limited by this.

Lastly, on the subject of timings, the length of the campaign is also important. Without rushing it, the shorter the fundraising campaign the better. This length depends on the homework done beforehand and the number of effective people on hand to get out there and solicit. My preference would be for six weeks with an allowance of another month for follow up. This requires constant pushing and maintenance of momentum. Keeping the effort on a high is not easy but it is considerably better than allowing the whole thing to flounder and sink into a quagmire. Enthusiasm, example, sustained effort, accountability and forcefulness, all while maintaining the loyalty and respect of everyone working hard on the project, are essential. It takes a good person to do this but the rewards are always worth it.

And a PS. Time itself can prove to be on your side or against it. It can help create and foster momentum, develop a bandwagon effect and build a crescendo of excitement when the end is in sight and the goal close to being accomplished. On the other hand, when things don't seem to be moving forward positively or at the required pace, it can make the goal appear unrealistic or even insurmountable. This is the testing time; the regeneration time; the opportunity for renewed leadership. It is the critical time and will not come again. Either we move on or we stop and collapse. There is really no option because, like the dream and vision that fired up the project in the first place, nothing will happen without it. And so, it has to be this same dream and vision that brings back the desire, drive and enthusiasm to re-generate the effort and substantiate the perennial truth that espouses: "The only time is now."

What to ask for?

Whether or not a fundraising team should consider telling a prospective donor what amount to give is the subject of much discussion. In the majority of cases, the donor will be glad to hear you suggest a given amount or a sensible guideline. In a few cases, they will take umbrage at being put into the same box as others or limited in what they may choose to do. Do remember that it is still better to come away with $50 than demand $100 and receive nothing. Much depends on the degree of rapport established and the respective personality types. This takes discernment because half the time the actual amount sought can be increased!

Governmental involvement

For a large community project, governmental investment at the local level will probably become essential. In most cases, especially for the main capital expense involved with site preparation and building (and possibly land acquisition), the two principal ways will include either property tax or sales tax. Both of these will require a strong approval from property owners and voters. But don't expect either method to be easily achieved, unless the following is worked on beforehand:

1. A good local fundraiser to show that a lot of people are already behind it.
2. Thought and deliberation concerning the implications and ramifications of sales tax or property tax increases.
3. In the case of sales tax (generally considered the best way to go), some creative thinking which could, perhaps, combine this capital project with one or more other initiatives.

4. Calculations that would show that this measure is a temporary one, like one half % increase for 5 years and then sunsetted.
5. Willingness to help with the “selling” of this initiative and associated smaller fundraiser to raise money for promotional literature and paid ads to do so.
6. Involvement of all sections of the community in such a way that there is “something for everybody” in the formula.
7. Recruitment of partnerships. For instance, could a portion of the grounds be the future site of a botanical garden? Is there a wetlands or wildlife area that the Division of Wildlife could adopt? Could the local Veterans organization have their flagpoles there? Can the school district utilize the facility? Can any of the features be tied into other governmental agencies? Could walkways be built to connect with a river walk system or park system? How can it be integrated into a current or future city or county master plan?

These are just ideas. The objective is to get as many partners as possible connected with, or involved with the present and future uses of the project.

Churches

From everyone to whom much has been given, much will be required. Luke 12:48

Like good stewards of the manifold grace of God, serve one another with whatever gift each of you has received. 1 Peter 4: 10

In addressing this subject, I am mindful of the fact that "Church" implies association with the Christian faith. However, I do not intend that this subject exclude any other faiths or traditions. If the ideas presented here can be adapted to other ways of managing funds within any other "Church", then I am pleased to present these words for consideration, if appropriate.

It is still tricky ground because different faiths, and denominations within them, have their own methods of collecting money. But all do it in order to sustain a working budget. And, in reality, a certain amount of money has to be raised each year or the Church will end that year with a deficit, or, worse still, be unable to pay their salaries or expenses. Some Church bodies are able to handle this because they have built up surpluses in previous years designed to see them through in a sparse year. Or they may have a foundation or endowment, which can assist. Others can rely on a few good people to bail them out. But most Churches, however, worry about the end result and often come to a point in the fall when both their planning and their faith are tested.

In no way do I intend, here, to tell any particular Church how to operate. If it is entirely faith based without a budget, that is fine, because, in many cases, this has been proved to work.

If it is through a strong pledge campaign where a financial committee figures in a percentage for members of the congregation not coming through because of death, moving to another community or just being dissatisfied with the Church, that, too, is OK. They may also be able to count on some new members joining and contributing financially. They may also be able to figure, historically, what has traditionally come in, in plate offerings from those who do not pledge and from visitors. Pledges and tithes are at the core of Church survival and neither necessarily come naturally. Both require a considerable commitment, which is often given, regardless of current economic conditions. Hopefully, these methods will work, but in practice, there is often a shortfall unless addressed in a timely fashion.

In many of the larger denominations, pamphlets and books on the subject are printed and updated with new ideas, as well as several time-tested methods, which have been used for decades. Unfortunately, congregations get tired of the "same old stuff" and today's fast pace and rate of accelerating change almost demand innovative strategies in order to rejuvenate the statistical and traditional methods of getting worshipers to continually give more. Methods like "stepping up to the next rung on the ladder" or door-to-door presentations of "the package" are OK in some circumstances but hardly advisable for adoption year after year. Instead, a closer look at the demographics and emphasis on priorities becomes more important. Above all, the way in which the need for money is presented, becomes the defining factor.

My suggestions, based on my own experience over the years, are designed to offer some practical tips, which have a reasonably good chance of working:

1. It is wise for the Pastor to involve him/herself in the financial health of the Church and learn to read and understand financial reports. This includes cash flow

analysis and history of giving within that Church body over the last few years. It is too late to suddenly be faced with a lack of funds when the picture could have been forecast earlier.

2. It is equally important that the Pastor personally addresses the subject of money and preaches about it at least two or three times during the year. The Bible does, after all, mention money many times and Jesus uses it in His teachings and parables. Money is not a dirty word or one which is beneath the status of the pulpit. It is a part of our society, religious or not, and without it, very little functions. In the right circumstances, the subject of money, Church needs and salaries for Pastor, staff, utilities and maintenance, is absolutely respectable.

3. Many people who give to Churches, tithe. This is good and involves commitment and discipline on their part. It creates a scenario where money given to the Church, Synagogue, Temple, Mosque, Fellowship or Body of Christ comes off the top. I.e.: it is given first, before anything else. To increase the number of people who tithe and the amount they give takes serious motivating techniques, education and explanation of the Biblical principles of giving and receiving. This, again, has to be done jointly by the Pastor and/or a financial committee head, who can either motivate and speak well him/herself or can get someone else (preferably well known and highly respected within the Church body) to do so.

4. Although, ideally, many people who give to Churches genuinely give out of devotion, tradition, loyalty and love, not all giving is completely unconditional. In fact, lets face it, very little, is. When people look at what their money is going towards, they can question anything from the Pastor's salary package to the need for a new sound system or musical instruments for the youth. They may even be skeptical about some missionary projects abroad or money that is going to the next higher level of that Church's administration. It is not often realized that most people will not complain openly but that their desire to give is definitely modified by what they consider to be important and prudent. If a few people complain, you can be certain that they are probably voicing those misgivings on behalf of a much larger silent number. In other words, they need to be convinced that their hard earned money is being wisely used on essentials and not on wasteful projects or grand schemes. Justification for expenditures is extremely important and always needs to be open to review. This is even more an issue for those who are business people or whose own packages are dependent on that business's capacity to pay them. The same goes for the elderly who see their own spending power diminish because of rising medical and other costs and compare this situation with a Church budget which has just increased by, say, 8%.

5. One of the best ways to increase giving is to take certain capital expense items out of the general budget and convert them to special needs projects. Examples might include things like a Church van or major repairs to it, new floor coverings, children's Bible school supplies, a new copier, Church camps, computer equipment, musical instruments and their maintenance and even heating and cooling bills. By doing this, the budget looks less, becomes more realistic and is therefore more sellable. It is not deceiving because it is stating, up front, that these special project items are other opportunities for individuals to underwrite or pay for, according to their own priorities and means, **after and in addition to their regular contributions**. Also, when people just give, as in the case of a tithe, they lose control of where their money is going. Some will, of course, be able to reconcile this by telling themselves to just think it is “all God’s work” or “the Ministry.” That is fine. But others will likely be more inclined to devote their finances to what they can rationalize as a real need, here and now; one that is tangible and one that they can literally buy into.

6. All of these things, listed above, as well as lots of other special project spending can be spread over the course of the year (not all at one time), as special needs, which require separate assistance. This enables the many “special interests” within the Church to support their own particular priority and provides them the chance to take credit for coming to the rescue of that area of need. It also encourages the anonymous giver to step up to the plate and provide a substantial gift, for which they gain a different kind of satisfaction, as well as, a year end tax advantage. The main thing here is to clearly publicize the need, vocally, in bulletins and newsletters and with sign up sheets displayed within the Church, ideally with someone seated at a table with aids like a picture or thermometer or poster showing the whys and wherefores. And by the way, don’t underestimate the potential giving power of those who are on the distribution list for newsletters but who seldom actually attend a service. They may well feel that they can fulfill their contract with God and the Church by writing a check in response to a stated important need. Don’t be shy in coming out with a statement like: “This church is appreciative of the time, talents and resources that so many people contribute. If you are able (or feel led) to help us with the following wants and needs, you will be helping us all in a wonderful and tangible way! Thank you all.”

7. Some Churches send out statements to people who have tithed or pledged. This is a good idea. Once a quarter is probably the best time but to be most effective, it should be accompanied by a note (which stands out) indicating the continuing need and asking politely but firmly for those who are behind, to catch up. It can also ask those "who have been especially blessed", to do their best to come up with a little extra.

8. For some reason, Churches as a whole, are not always the best at saying thank you. Sometimes this is because the system prohibits (in theory), the Pastor or financial committee from knowing who gives what. This is unfortunate but to be respected. But there still needs to be a way to convey thanks to individuals who are loyal and generous, and especially thank those who come up with even more to help with special needs. The best way of achieving this is to design a short personal note that accompanies the statement or that can be sent out separately. The cost of the postage stamp and small amount of effort will result in good feelings all round and do much to set the stage for further giving. The note can say something like this:

Dear ___________,

We, the Church, Pastor and Finance Committee, acknowledge your kind and generous gift of $....... for (our special needs project).

Thank you so much for your contribution. It is people like you who help make it happen and we are so grateful for your response and action.

In Christ's love.

(Signed by the Pastor or financial chair or lay leader), but if this is not deemed suitable, it can be signed by the treasurer or the person who handles the checks and makes the deposits.

9. One more item is worth considering seriously. If statements are sent out quarterly, givers will get them in early April, July, October and January. The last one will arrive too late to push for that last Christmas and end-of-year drive (to help balance the budget). Therefore, this last statement needs to be sent out to reflect the giving position of both the individual and the Church as a whole, so that it arrives in people's homes in early December.

10. The final and most important requirement is for the Church itself to be completely on top of its financial position and be able and willing to tell it as it is. Just printing a set of numbers in the bulletin or newsletter is not enough. A lot of people don't relate to numbers and will assume that all is OK because no one has indicated otherwise. Therefore, if there is a crunch time, (usually known by October), this fact has to be revealed. It need not be conveyed or perceived as a failure or unduly negative but merely a truthful reality. Having stated this factual situation in a way that everyone can understand, which entails a short, strong presentation at service times, the next things to be articulated are: "This is what we need" and "This is what we are asking you to do, so that jointly, with God's help, we can solve the problem and do it before it becomes a crisis." In other words, create a giving opportunity, which serves both the needs of being fiscally prudent and also calls on faith to answer, through the love and generosity of the congregation.

11. If, say, by November, there is still a projected shortfall (allowing for historically based expectations for the month of December), the next move is a delicate one. It needs to be presented to the Church body as a graphic picture of the current deficit and ramifications for the end of the year. And with this situation, it should list some of the areas like salaries, staff hours, programs, important repairs and maintenance etc, which very likely will have to be cut. This gesture, is, after all, no different than any small business owner faces or anyone else running a household budget. It is the way in which this message is crafted that is the key. There should be no guilt conveyed or projected, and no threat imparted. In fact the tone should remain optimistic and subtly state that this is not an unusual occurrence at this time of the year. In the end, it is a matter of leadership and motivation. Above all, the need has to be clearly stated to the whole congregation. It is not much use if the finance committee knows very well what the position is and continues to passively accept a declining situation. Nor is it a good idea to suddenly announce that because of the serious deficit, it has become necessary to make the following cuts, effective immediately! This last course of action is bound to upset many in the congregation and could even split the Church because of cuts, which are not perceived to be impartial.

12. Not surprisingly, even in the worst circumstances, there are many people that will contribute extra money and re-prioritize their giving strategy because they understand and can empathize with a straightforward need. Indeed, they are happy to come to the rescue. This type of giving not only provides great satisfaction for "a job well done" but also involves their active participation in the solution and leaves the Church with a fresh new approach for the next year. No one likes to see their place of worship bogged down with the inheritance of a deficit for which different levels of blame are attached, resulting in a less than truly Christian atmosphere of love and respect.

13. The postscript to all of this is, once again, a thank you to all who give. We know that it is not how much a person or family unit gives so much as their motive, commitment and follow through. It would be nice to assume that all giving requires no acknowledgement or recognition, and this may be true or even correct for some givers and many of those who tithe or pledge consistently, but in the cases of special projects or year end appeals, it is entirely appropriate for those who have made the extra effort to support their Church, to be personally thanked by the Pastor and/or the finance committee chair or other designated person who can speak "on behalf of our whole Church body."

14. More than ever before, the financial needs of the Church require explanation. The Pastor and the financial committee, elders, Church Council, Trustees and all in authority must keep abreast of the likely expenses for the current and next year. Budgets are becoming more and more important. Control of them is even more important. If income is down, only two things should happen: the first is that the congregation should be informed and an appeal made to catch up. Apart from clear, strong announcements made at service times and in the bulletin and newsletter, a simple note, inserted in the holder space at the back of the pews or seating, can be placed at the appropriate times. It should say something on the lines of: "In response to our budgeted financial needs and special ministries for this year, I/we would like to increase my/our giving by contributing this extra amount now and/or increase my/our pledge (estimate of giving), from $------ to $-----. Signed (with printed name) and date." The second thing is that cuts be considered, announced ahead of time and, if money has not come in, implemented. Even a Church has to learn to live within its means!

Grants

A grant is not a handout. It should be regarded more as a financial endorsement for a good project that is already well under way in its planning, fundraising and satisfaction of benefits to the community.

There are several categories of grants. Many are available only for certain geographical areas, certain types of programs or particular agencies. These are normally fairly narrow in scope and can be extremely detailed. Entities like city or county can apply for grants specific to municipal subjects or buildings. Churches or city/county agencies or institutions like museums and historical societies can apply for things like historical preservation grants or archival research. Schools may also benefit from being able to apply directly or indirectly for relevant programs or refurbishment of old buildings. While it may appear that all of these are not in the slightest bit relevant to this book's purpose, I mention them because there are people out there who are constantly engaged in grant writing, right there, in your own small community. Try to find out who they are. Some will be most helpful and even be willing to share their skills to assist.

Other agencies with a good history of operating in the community or nearby, will include Hospice, Partners, Resource Centers, Boys and Girls Clubs, etc. Once again, there is normally a staff member or Director whose job it is to search out relevant grant possibilities and fill out the paperwork. Their resource list, if they are willing to share it, is a valuable tool.

Now we come to everyone else. The problem is that "everyone else" is a huge number of deserving organizations, all of which seem to start out by asking, "Why don't we go for a grant?" Well, we need to be realistic here and try to understand a few basic facts:

1. There are always far more grant seekers than there are private or public foundations or Fed/State moneys to go around.
2. In the case of foundations, which do give out money, their ability to do so can be predicated on the state of the current market economy and, in some cases, their own ability to secure additional contributions. In the late 1990s when things were good and booming, returns on foundations' investments may have exceeded more than 10% or 12%. In the first three years of this new millennium, many investment returns were in the very low single digits or even in negative territory with the actual principal value ending up at less than the year before. Some foundations lost 25% or more of their overall value and this obviously affected their available disbursements.
3. As a general rule, foundations are only allowed to give out grant money out of investment income. Most have to, by law, disperse at least 4% of their corpus (principal), although this figure can be carried over in certain circumstances.
4. The number of grant applications coming into the more well-known foundations is increasing all the time, to the extent that their staff may not even have time to review all of them thoroughly. Therefore, they are having to adopt techniques which save time by filtering out large numbers of applications based on inadequate answers to fundamental questions and minor technicalities.

5. A typical grant application takes a lot of time to complete and may call for follow up reports and additional paperwork.
6. Competition is fierce so it is essential that you are a strong match with the interests and objectives of the particular foundation that you are applying to.
7. Notwithstanding the above, the total amount of money in US foundations today is more than it has ever been and while they may not be able to give out a much as they did in, say, 2001, it is still probably double what it was ten years ago.

Qualities required

If you are even considering a grant, there are two ways of going about it: either employ a professional grant writer and pay for it, or do it yourself. Either way, these are the qualities required:

Extreme patience, determination, perseverance, attention to detail, ability to collate accurately, understand facts and figures, convey information succinctly and dynamically, read and understand financial reports, balance sheets, budgeting and profit and loss statements, and remain focused in a logical and left brained fashion.

If you feel you don't have these qualities, now is the time to try something else!

Even if you are the proud owner of all these characteristics, you still have to be good at accepting rejection and turn downs, knowing that the application process may take several weeks or months, be reviewed only once a year and exhaust much of your time, energy and resources. But it does build endurance and experience!

It has been said that grant writing is a true art. But it definitely takes real action and it should be understood at the outset that grant money should only constitute a portion of the whole cost of the project. Generally speaking, a foundation that gives out money will want to see their contribution as an investment, which shows a positive return. They will not want to see their money going to administration costs and will frown on any organization that shows these costs to be 50% or more. Instead they are likely to be far more favorably impressed if administrative costs are significantly less. For this to happen it may be necessary to be somewhat creative with accounting. I do not mean a fabrication of the books but rather a close look at the various line items attributed to administration. For example, if vehicle and gas expenses or certain amounts of time are all earmarked as general overhead administrative expense, the percentage will be much higher than if some of these expenses are put against a particular program of service. In the case of a paid executive director, this is very important because it may be possible to split his/her salary down into several components, some of which are <u>not</u> administration. So do bear in mind that donated monies are primarily meant to go to help the people that you serve and not, merely, to keep the door open.

I am trying not to be too negative here but below is a list showing the type of questions that may have to be answered – taken from a current Denver based Foundation.

KENNETH KENDAL KING FOUNDATION

Please follow our format, include the exact paragraph numbers and titles and enclose original and five copies of the proposal.

1. Name of organization
2. Address, telephone number and fax number
3. Name and title of person submitting the application
4. The mission of your non-profit
5. When and where was your organization founded?
6. Please state how your organization is governed/managed.
7. The amount requested and submission date of request
8. Describe how and when the funds will be used.
9. Are there any time requirements for the distribution of the funds requested?
10. How does the organization receive its basic financial support?
11. Does the organization receive any Federal, State or local government financing or funding?
    a. Government entities supplying financing or funding
    b. Date and amount of *each* government funding and its percentage of budget
    c. Will funding continue?
12. List other Foundation support for this project or other projects of your organization. volunteers in your programs or projects?
13. If applicable, how many persons on an average benefit from your services in one year?
14. How many employees, including staff, are on your payroll?
15. Special attention is given to your financial presentation.
    a. Provide your current budget, balance sheet and income and expense statement for the past two years. *Grant requests omitting* the *above will be denied.*
    b. Provide your most recent audit report.
    c. Provide amount in percentages spent on administrative support, fund raising and program services.
16. Include a list of your Board of Directors with their business and professional positions.
17. 1t is *mandatory* that a *copy of* the *501* (c)(3) in the legal *name of* the *organization applying for* a *grant be included*
18. Have you previously applied for a grant from the King Foundation?
    a. If so, when?
    b. Dates and amounts received
    c. Declined?
19. How did you learn about the Kenneth Kendal King Foundation')

Completed guidelines *(original and five copies)* should be submitted to the Kenneth Kendal King Foundation

Understanding the components of a classic proposal

The cover letter

This is usually one page and is written after the main proposal is completed. It should be written on organization letterhead and signed by the board chair or executive director. It needs to arouse interest in the reviewer and make them want to continue. It should include an introduction of the applicant organization, reason(s) for approaching the donor, statement of need or project/program, brief outline of the plan, amount requested and time frame, and a sentence thanking the funder for considering the request.

The Executive Summary

The length can vary between one paragraph and a whole page. It is a critical section and often determines whether the reader starts to take an active interest or becomes turned off. Like the cover letter, this is best written after completing the main proposal. It has to concisely summarize the whole proposal and may reiterate part of the cover letter. It must include evidence of the organization's expertise and capacity to carry out the project, it's purposes, activities, and accomplishments. It also needs to outline the nature of the need or problem that your organization is addressing, together with the proposed solution, description of the project plan and amount requested. Spend time on this because it needs to be dynamically appealing.

The Narrative

The narrative normally consists of six sections:

1. Problem/project need statement (a few paragraphs to one page).

Background information relating to the need that the organization is addressing.
Facts, statistics, anecdotes and other evidence to support the need. Try to paint a picture of an accurate but worthwhile need that is pertinent and useful to the community. Demonstrate that the scope of the project is within the organization's ability to adequately address. Above all, show what the project, if funded, will do.

2. Project Description (can be up to three pages).

This is the nuts and bolts section. It needs to show exactly, in sufficient detail, what the project consists of and how it will come about. Timings, positive benefits and who will be coordinators and managers of the project are important, as are goals, objectives and methods. Show staffing structure, administrative details and timings for project start and completion. Also include the vision behind the request and why you think it is really important and why you think it can work.

3. Organizational information (up to one page).

This section can be embedded at this point or it can be placed at the beginning, before the need statement. It should include the history of the organization, its goals, mission statement, governing structure, primary activities, constituents and accomplishments. (This is a good place to insert some media coverage showing past and current activities).

4. Clear statement of request (one paragraph).

How much are you requesting? From whom? For what purpose and under what time frame?

5. Conclusion (one to two paragraphs).

This section recaps the main proposal in a passionate way, which stirs interest and ties into a bigger picture that includes future visions, follow-up and benefits of being able to implement the project plan. It is your last opportunity to generate sympathy and empathy. This final plea can carry a lot of weight.

6. Budget (one page).
This section must show a financial breakdown of the project and has to provide details showing current assets, projected income and expenses, including the ability to maintain the project in the future. Other funding sources should be shown and especially, the amount of money already raised or provided by local means or organizational savings. Remember to give figures for the time and numbers of volunteer help. This alone, can account for several thousands of dollars, which can be shown as income against appropriate expenses. It also gives value to your organization and demonstrates support from outside the board and any paid staff. Explanatory notes are often necessary, as are evidence of past and current financial viability, further plans to enhance capital and other activities designed to support the project.

Grant Writing Tips

- Before starting the proposal, be absolutely clear about what it is you want to accomplish. When is it needed by? Who will be responsible for it? What will it cost? What resources in your organization make you a suitable contender? Who benefits?
- Research potential funders. Are you a match? Find out who they have funded before and

whether or not their interests and priorities are compatible with your project.

- Look at the guidelines. Study them in great detail. Can your project fit?
- Get hold of and read the foundation's last annual report. Look for what they have funded recently and try to get a feel for how they think.
- Study the amounts that have been funded and tailor your request to fit these criteria.
- Spend time considering exactly how your program or project might interest them.
- Try to actually speak to a grant officer beforehand and get a few tips.
- Tell your story in a compelling way. Demonstrate a well thought-out plan. Show how it will make a difference.
- Keep it simple. Show that the project will succeed and is based on clearly laid out, supportable facts. Use the right words, concisely.
- Avoid jargon, be honest, don't exaggerate and don't promise more than you can deliver
- In all dealings, both written and verbal, show passion for your organization and its goals and aspirations. Present enthusiastically!
- Don't forget to thank the funder – several times!
- Even if you are turned down, keep the foundation on your mailing list.
- Regardless of success or not, send them periodic reports, even when they are not required.

If all of this looks too daunting, bear in mind that it is equally so for other applicants. The process is designed to filter out the weaker organizations. But even so, many organizations still get grants and the odds are in the region of 10% to 15%, but can increase significantly with good planning, foundation research and religious following of the application's guidelines. So time spent weighing up the amount of work involved, versus the possibility of a positive result is well spent. In doing this, four more factors should be taken into account:

The imperatives

1. Contact the Foundation first and feel them out concerning their projected grant dispensation for next year.
2. Ask about dates for completed applications. It is no use starting out in July for an application that has to be in by September 15th if it turns out that it will take four months to get all the relevant info to complete.
3. Make sure, beforehand, that the object of the grant (e.g. a capital project), is, in fact, within the grant criteria. Some foundations will only give up to 25% of the cost of a capital project and require the first 75% to already be in place. There is nothing more debilitating than doing six weeks work, only to find out, after submission, that buried in the small print was a sentence that precluded capital projects altogether and that this foundation only gave money to programs and studies.
4. Let's say that you are going for a $500 grant. Would it be quicker, easier and less painful to get ten people to come up with $50 each? Lets further add that if you value your time at $20 an hour and it takes 50 hours of work to put it together, let alone another 10 hours to complete the "after the award" paperwork, is it really worth it?

Contacts and other Sources

Although they may not give substantial sums of money, it is always worth contacting some of your local utility companies and the big box retailers. Some of these, like an electric, long distance or local telephone carrier, cable company or natural gas supplier, may have a fund or foundation from which they disperse small grants on a monthly basis within their service areas. Others may do this semi annually or at one time during the year. There will be forms to fill out and, possibly, a board meeting to attend but a $200 or $500 check is well worth going for and occasionally, they will ask for more details and single you out for a larger donation.

Each state or larger community will have an organization that specializes in putting on seminars which can help and provide contacts for some of the foundations that are applicable, together with guidelines. Such organizations may also publish an annual Grants Guide, both in written form and on line. This may entail a fee but it is an excellent starting point. In Colorado, one of the current organization is Community Resource Center, 655 Broadway, Suite 300, Denver, CO 80203-3426. Their telephone number is 800 516 6284 or 303 623 1540 Their web address is www.crcamerica.org and their Email address is info@ crcamerica.org.

In the summer of 2003, Community Resource Center will be introducing an exciting national initiative, which will focus on helping non-profit groups become more effective. This program is called NPower Colorado and will include a free web-based clearinghouse of information, related to the effective use of technology by non-profits. There will be planning sessions, workshops and general assistance given to enhance local expertise and resource locating.

Another development that has recently come about (in Colorado), is the adoption by most local foundations, of a new standardized form called the Colorado Common Grant Application. Excellent information on this and many other associated links is available from the web by just typing in "Colorado common grant application."

Some useful on line contacts are:

Fdncenter.org
Grantstation.com
Chronicle of philanthropy.org
Fundraiserstation.com
Efundraising.com
High-tech-fundraiser.com
Fundraisingdepot.com
Cravercreative.com
Nonprofit.about.com
Fundraising.com
Aromalightcandles.com
Kma.com
1-fundraisers-fundraising.com
hometowntrivia.com
non-profit-fundraising.com
abcfundraising.comscratchhandhelp.com
Fundraising-ideas.com
Hgpfundraising.com
Hersheyfundraising.comPermamark.com

Here are two software options:

Fundraising.org
Fundraisersoftware.com

Two good books on the subject are "Getting Funded: A Complete Guide to Proposal Writing" by Mary Hall, and "Grassroots Grants" by Andy Robinson.

I cannot vouch for any of the above but, if you have the time, there are lots to choose from and some pretty novel ideas, all of which require money!

One more worthwhile use of anyone's time, especially if they are interested in learning more about grants, foundations and their giving strategies, is to attend a locally sponsored

Philanthropy Days event. These excellent programs are usually one or two-day seminars and take place several times a year throughout the state. They try to cover all the regional base communities and bring in experts in appropriate fields and some of the actual foundation directors or persons who handle the grant applications. The events are normally underwritten by local businesses like banks and attract dozens of non-profits. If nothing else, they are a great place to network. And don't forget the lottery funds. The availability and usage of these funds will vary from state to state but they can be a major source of funds if your project can meet their current criteria. For Colorado, the contact is:

Great Outdoors Colorado (GOCO) in Denver.
303 226 4522/4523/4561.
www.goco.org or info@goco.org

These people do a great job of allocating large quantities of money throughout the state and they put on some excellent technical assistance workshops at regular intervals. However, one of their criteria is that all applications have to be submitted under the auspices of a municipal entity like city or county.

Conclusion.

In conclusion, be realistic, be able to satisfy all the questions and categories shown and be expert at clearly demonstrating your case with persuasion, showing the number of people served. Just "because it will help us and we desperately need it" is not enough. It has to be shown that your organization and project is something outstanding and that you already have lots of people behind you, have contributed yourselves and have monies, pledges, commitments and partnerships already lined up. Remember also, that going after grants should only be regarded as one part of a diversified plan.

And if you think this is like the proverbial chicken and egg, it is! The question is not whether your need is sincere so much as whether you can stay the course and provide the answers in the format which the foundation wants, and in such a manner that naturally brings your application to the top of the pile. Somehow, you must distinguish your organization from all the others. This will include going the extra mile.

The 501(c)(3)Organization

Not-for-profit does not mean that an organization should not try their hardest to produce more income than expenditures. The goal should always be to grow the bank account so that more services can be provided and, when a function makes a loss or expenses temporarily increase, there is enough reserve to not impede the main goals of the organization.

This section is designed only to act as a layman's simple interpretation of what can be a complex subject. In no way am I attempting to compete with attorneys or accountants, who are more qualified to offer professional advice and perform the necessary work. The object, here, is to give you some idea of the bigger picture and what is involved.

There are two groups of organizations that may find this of benefit. The first are ones who are already set up as a 501(c)(3) organization but whose board, officers and committee members have little idea of what that is because they were not responsible for setting it up and, in any case, may not be up to date on current rulings. The second category consists of newer organizations who see the need to get started on forming a 501 (c)(3) but do not know how to commence the procedure.

In reality, it should be noted that **not all organizations have** to become a 501(c)(3). The IRS may consider them to be tax exempt as they are. These organizations include:

Churches, church auxiliaries, and church associations.
Any organization that is a private foundation.
Any organization whose gross receipts for any tax-reporting year does not exceed $5,000.

This last one usually prohibits most organizations from not becoming a 501(c)(3).

However, there are distinct advantages for going to the trouble of becoming a 501(c)(3), and these include:

- Public recognition of exempt status.
- Advance assurance to donors of deductibility of contributions.
- Exemptions for certain state and federal excise taxes.
- Non-profit mailing privileges.

Which type of 501 organization?

Not unexpectedly, the IRS currently lists twenty five different types of 501(c) tax exempt organization categories, plus another five non (c) categories and a 527 category for political organizations. This can be confusing because, for example, a service club will be a 501(c)(4), and an agricultural or horticultural organization will be a 501(c)(5), but a religious organization will be a 501(c)(3), whereas a religious and apostolic association will be a 501(d). Confused? Don't worry! For the sake of this anticipated readership, I am only going to deal with the 501(c)(3) organization, with which most of us are familiar. For definition purposes, this refers to "charitable, religious, educational, scientific, etc organizations."

Quite simply, a 501(c)(3) is a federally recognized organization that allows you to collect money from other people who can claim a charitable contribution on their own tax return. Other 501s do not necessarily allow you to do that.

There are tens of thousands of 501(c)(3)s in existence. Every one is listed annually within the government and these lists can be down loaded or seen at local libraries. The establishment of a 501(c)(3) is not only advantageous from the point of view of obtaining contributions, it also adds a degree of credibility to your organization and shows that you are willing to step up to that league of well-established and better known organizations. Also, when applying for a grant, most foundations or government agencies will expect you to have your own 501(c)(3) organization and will not look so sympathetically on a request which is being processed under the umbrella of another (established) 501(c)(3).

One other thing to keep in mind is that should your organization ever have to disband, all assets held at the time, have, by law, to be transferred or handed over to another tax-exempt organization. You cannot just fold and distribute any remaining assets to people within that organization.

What to do to obtain IRS recognition of exemption

Step one is to obtain an EIN (Employer Identification Number), if you do not already have one. This is done on IRS Form SS-4.

The next step is to form a corporation. This should be a Not for Profit corporation and preferably filed in the state in which you are operating. This will allow you to be not subject to income tax. It will also state that you cannot pay any dividends to members. My advice is to use an attorney for this and the secret is to enlist one who is sympathetic to your cause. This should cut down on expenses and hopefully, result in a free (pro bono) contribution of his/her time and expertise.

After you have your Not for Profit corporation in place, you can commence the work necessary to apply for an IRS ruling that enables you to qualify as a 501(c)(3). Once again, it is advisable to use a friendly CPA as there is quite a lot of accounting work involved and it is important to get it right the first time. There used to be no fee for submission but as of 2003, it is now $250 and that amount could change.

The IRS forms needed to fully understand all of what can be involved are:

- Form 1023. Application of recognition for exemption with instructions and accompanying form 872-C.
- Form 8717. User fee and determination letter request.
- Publication 557. Tax exempt status of your organization. (a 60-page document!)
- Form 578. Tax information for Private Foundations and managers.

This last one is not so important because your organization will, in the vast majority of cases, be a public entity. (See paragraph on Foundations).

All necessary IRS forms can be obtained by calling 1 800 829 3676 or down loaded from www.irs.gov The State form is available from your local Secretary of State's office. In Colorado, this is 303 894 2200 Ext 2 (Business section) or 303 869 4860 (fax). Or from www.sos.state.co.us (Email address: sos.admin1@sos.state.co.us). The form is entitled "Articles for incorporation for a non-profit" (Form 300). The fee is $50 and it is a simple one-page document. Make sure you ask for and get the most current versions, as they change frequently.
For other States, use www.sos.state followed by the abbreviation of the State's name, followed by us. This works for most States but if it does not (as in the case of CA), just type in, on any search engine, Secretary of State California.(or appropriate State name).

The main application form (1023), will require you to provide detailed information on your activities and operations, show sources of financial support, describe your fundraising program, show names and addresses of members and the governing body, answer numerous technical requirements, complete financial statements for the current year and the three proceeding years (if you have been in existence for that time), fill in current balance sheets and file form 872-C which provides for a temporary recognition or advanced ruling period

As you can see, the complexity of this, combined with a $250 fee will immediately weed out any organization that is not well prepared or serious.

If these forms are filled in correctly, the tentative approval can come relatively quickly,(a few months), but it may take a year or more before final approved status is granted.

Filings and donor's tax advantages

A 501(c)(3) organization does not have to file an IRS return unless it's income for the year exceeds $25,000. Income is described as cash receipts. It does not matter if the income is $26,000 and the expenditures are $27,000. It is the actual income that dictates whether or not a return must be filed. And the amount of assets held is not of interest to the IRS. This number can continue to grow. If you do have to file, the form to use is IRS form 990 EZ for income up to $100,000 or form 990 if income is over $100,000.

For the donor, the benefits include the ability to claim tax relief on contributions made to the 501(c)(3) to the extent of their current tax bracket. For larger contributors, this may be about 28% of their contribution. For others it may be a little higher. However, now that the standard deduction amount has been raised, it may turn out that smaller donations will not be enough to get beyond the standard threshold amount, when itemized. This situation will differ with every individual donor.

If a donor contributes a physical item, the same will apply, except that any such item valued at $500 or more should be able to be of provable worth, either by way of a professional appraisal or other evidence clearly showing it's value. It is not the responsibility of the receiving organization to have to provide this but I do believe, that it is their duty to point this out to someone who wants to donate such an item.

In the case of stock or property donations, it is strongly recommended that this be discussed with the potential donor and a tax professional.

Foundations

I do not propose to delve into this in any depth because a foundation is usually perceived by the smaller organizations as a source of funds and not the solicitor, even though these foundations themselves are, of course, constantly working to secure additional funds and act as an agency for receiving tax-based contributions. The section on grants covers the other half of this subject.

One rather amazing fact is that US grant-making foundations increased their total assets in the year 2000 by 8.4 %. That additional amount is very close to a whopping $500 billion. This resulted in a record amount of giving in the following year (2001), to $29 billion. 2002 may not have been quite as good but the statistics indicate that foundation giving is still increasing and total assets continue to rise. Currently, there are close to 60,000 foundations in this country. Many of them have less than $10 million in assets.

There are two types of foundations: public and private. **A private foundation** such as the (Bill) Gates Foundation, is one in which an individual puts up the money and retains some control. They have to pay taxes. I only mention this category because many specialist financial companies and attorneys dealing with substantial estates are guiding clients towards the idea of setting up a small private foundation. This is both for tax benefits and for control of their giving, especially as it relates to the creation of a legacy. So it follows naturally that if there are people out there, in your own community, who have followed this route, they will be seeking and establishing policies which enable them to accomplish their personal objectives. This is why it is important to continually publicize your own cause or organization as a suitable recipient. One never knows what the future results may be if the right seeds are sown now. Remember, it does not take an unduly rich person to be sympathetic to your cause and devote a portion of their estate towards helping it.

A public foundation is one where all moneys received have come from many different individuals or other parties and is not controlled by one majority contributor. These do <u>not</u> have to pay taxes. They do, however, have to disburse at least 4% of the average of that year's assets, regardless of whether they have made money or not. This means that some have had to dip into their corpus (principle) in order to satisfy IRS requirements. Say, for example, a foundation had a net worth of $100,000 and was able to receive investment income of $3,000 for the year but no further contributions. Their year end worth would be $103,000 and they would be obliged to hand out 4% of their average worth, which is $101,500 or $4060, which would leave them with only $98,940. If they go ahead and report these disbursements, they will not have to pay any taxes. If they do not disburse the 4%, they will have to pay taxes. The reason I bring up this subject is for you to know that all public foundations do have to give out money and someone is going to get it!

Community Foundations

Sometimes a well-established public foundation can be used to "house" charitably derived funds. This is especially valid in the case of a proposed endowment fund. The advantages of this are three-fold:

1. It takes time, resources, money and considerable expertise to set up and run an endowment.
2. A small endowment will likely invest monies in standard, safe vehicles, which may end up costing them 2% or 3% in administrative fees. A larger community foundation will quite possibly handle all the paperwork involved for 1% or even less.
3. A community foundation is likely to already have larger funds and is therefore able to negotiate better rates of return on their investments.

Naturally, there are many ramifications, not the least of which is the matter of control. But, for the most case, having a larger foundation look after the assets of a smaller organization under the auspices of "pass through" funds and/or "donor designated" funds, may well save a lot of time and expense and be relatively easy to manage. As an added bonus, the larger foundation will have much greater expertise in matters relating to gift annuities, pooled income funds, unitrusts, bequests and stock or property transactions. At any rate, it is worth inquiring to see if there are community foundations in existence in your area and talking to them about a joint venture like this. The latest trend nationally, is headed towards the use of community foundations. Many of the smaller established private foundations are, themselves, beginning to transfer their assets to these community foundations.

Endowments themselves

An endowment is a foundation that provides income over a period of time. It can only use its interest or appreciated income and it does not touch the principle. So, for example, lets say that an endowment has $200,000 and averaged an 8% income over a number of years, it could give out $16,000 a year. This would result in gifts valued at more than its principle worth in less than 13 years while still retaining the $200,000. All gifts donated to an endowment are done so knowing that the principle is retained in perpetuity.

Ideally, every Not for Profit organization should consider an endowment. This can be especially important for churches and entities who have to constantly fundraise in order to meet a percentage of their annual budget. The advantages include the fact that stable income is possible and that this additional income to any organization will help alleviate the stress placed on these entities because of having to do so many annual fundraisers. It will also be appreciated by many individuals and businesses who are hit hard on a constant basis from many of these same organizations. To the giver, an endowment provides a vehicle for the donor to think in terms of a "legacy." This becomes more and more important when people start to get serious about estate planning.

I recommend that when an endowment is set up, ten to fifteen per cent of all money received over a previously agreed upon sum, from the proceeds of special events and other fundraisers, be set aside and channeled into the endowment. For example: A fundraiser goal is $10,000. The event produces $11,000. $1,000 goes to the endowment. Or even if the event produces $9,000, I would still recommend that, say, $500 goes to the endowment. It has been shown many times that the growth of an endowment is exponential. The most difficult phase is at the beginning, when it is being got off the ground. Later, when it becomes more visible and well known (because it is being seen to give out small

amounts of money to the cause), it will start to grow and become credible. After that, there will be a good chance that, with the right encouragement, people will start to think about it when revising their estate planning.
If you are able to set up an endowment and/or work with a community foundation, the next step is to publicize it. A brochure is a valuable aid. So, too, is the placement of this type of information. Attorneys and accountants' offices are excellent places, as are doctor's offices. Better still, try to acquaint all professional who handle estate planning in your area, to become aware of your organization and what it does for the community. Lastly, recognize large donors to the endowment.

Some smaller communities have devised the idea of producing a combination brochure which has a heading like: "Ways to give to our community" It can then list all of the local foundations and endowments with a brief description of their respective purposes and goals. Once again, sensible distribution of these brochures is most important if they are to get the attention of possible donors. Wills and bequests are the ways in which all of these funds will start to grow significantly. The emphasis is always on the **legacy** that many community-minded individuals would like to leave. Our job is to make these opportunities easily available by publicizing the ways in which they can plan their giving strategies. And yes, these ways include us!

Some useful sources of help

National: The Foundation Center in New York.
212 807 3601 or 3623.
www.fdncenter.org

Colorado: Community Research Center in Denver
303 623 1540.
www.crcamerica.org

Colorado: Western Colorado Community Foundation.
970 243 3767.
www.wc-cf.org

See also the contacts in the grants section.

I again emphasize that this section is provided from an amateur's perspective. No responsibility is taken for absolute accuracy as defined by law or the IRS. In all cases, the appropriate professionals should be consulted to insure best results.

Professional consultants and organizers

Beware of the person who sells on promises. It is the result that counts, and all too often, this is not known until after the fee has been paid.

Many organizations pay for a special events coordinator. This decision has to be evaluated seriously. In some cases it is absolutely necessary. This is because that organization may have to put on an event or other form of fundraiser several times a year or even more frequently. Although many volunteers may be involved, this person holds down the base and provides continuity, especially for clerical support, telephone contact and general coordination. In cases like this, the coordinator may be a full time employee or part time. If he or she is good, they will take a lot of pressure off of the local director or person who is employed to actually run the various programs, manage a budget and supervise other staff. The key is to find the right person; one who can become the interface between the host organization and the fundraising volunteers, help with goal setting and dates, convene meetings and handle the paperwork. Such a person can be worth double his/her salary.

On the other hand, it is not always beneficial to have one giant function which raises $50,000 if the cost of putting it on is $35,000 and the special events coordinator is paid $12,000 for several months work, resulting in a huge amount of effort for a net gain of $3,000.

Every now and again an organization becomes tempted to bring in a paid outsider or professional fundraising company. Occasionally this may be a reasonable idea but, as in the case of nearly all consultants, their fee is high, their package looks slick and impressive and they tend to blind the innocent with their egos and apparent expertise. What they don't normally do is actually go out and physically collect money for you. They merely put together the package in a bright shiny folder cover and evaluate the community. Perhaps I am being a bit hard but the message is clear: Whoever you use, and whatever method you employ, you still have to get out there and ask. Of course, there are exceptions. Perhaps a five-year economic development long-range plan may merit a professional who can produce a number of referrals stating his/her effectiveness. And the selling of a school bond to the community may well benefit from an expert in that field. But in general, be wary. The result may well not justify the means or the costs involved.

Advantages

1. Objectivity. They may have special experience of dealing with several other towns of the same size and can present current, effective working techniques. They can look beyond local politics and personalities.
2. The specifications and statistics they produce will definitely support the goal of the endeavor and, for some givers, this type of well-presented information will be impressive enough to make them respond positively.
3. A professionally produced brochure and a plan for raising funds can be very helpful to a board, which has little experience or desire to actually solicit themselves.

Disadvantages

1. The cost is very high, often in tens of thousands of dollars. This can result in percentages as high as 30% or more. This means that for every $1,000 raised, only $700 will go to the

cause. This alone means that the goal would have to be set 30% higher than the figure originally calculated.

2. Having produced the fact sheets and figures, they will probably want a lot <u>more</u> money to assist with the actual task of supervising the raising of funds, making calls and doing the more important visitations.

3. If they do negotiate as in 2. above, the response will definitely not be so good as when local well-known personalities do it.

4. To many, the so-called pros will tend to come over as too smooth, arrogant and "big city." This will turn some people off. They may also not be willing to really listen to what local people are saying when they are asked for input.

5. Most importantly, they will tend to erode the position and responsibility of the board, who should be the most visible element of the whole operation. If a board thinks that they do not have to do their part because they are paying a professional to perform the task, they are wrong and will be sorely disappointed.

Saying Thank you

Gratitude is something that we express twice; once for receiving the gift and once to the person who gave it.

Don't need to read this? OK, but you may just be denying yourself the chance of a greater return. The fact is that this simple act is far more than just a formality or plain good manners. It is absolutely essential and the way in which it is done could affect the outcome of the immediate project and all others to follow. Indeed, thank yous need to be done in different ways, more than once, and completely personally and sincerely.

As with all good fundraising techniques, it takes time, effort, good memory and money. One thing is certain though; it is always beneficial and often highly productive. Here are some ways in which thank yous should be given:

To a silent auction donor or giver of physical items or gift certificates

- Thanks at the time the commitment is given.
- Thanks given when the item is picked up or delivered.
- Thanks shown in the bid sheet to the donor.
- Thanks given by the MC or organizer when making announcements at the function.
- Thanks, preferably written, after the function.
- Thanks to the donor, verbally, by all members of the board or committee as/when they bump into that

person on the street or elsewhere, like in a restaurant or social function.

- Within the framework of the thank you should be an explanation of how important the gift was, the interest it created, how the auction proceeds made all the difference in achieving the goal and a reiteration of the benefits to the community.

To help make this duty effective, it is a good idea to type out a list of all donors and what they donated and give it to everybody involved with the fundraiser. Each person should be told how important it is to express thanks, even if it means going a little out of their way. You can be sure that if a donor receives several acknowledgements of his/her gift, they will be most gratified and ready to respond immediately to the next request. The opposite is true if they get no recognition at all. Every thank you must be delivered positively and with enthusiasm.

<u>More "thank you's"</u>

People who send in membership dues should be thanked. This small gesture should be done promptly and will make them feel appreciated. It will also act as a receipt. This is a good opportunity to include any update or other information that you wish to impart concerning future activities.

Thanks need to be constantly given to the media, especially if they are willing to print auction items and include who donated them. This is, of course, much appreciated by business donors and goes a long way towards helping to promote the project.

Another form of thanking people is to compose a newspaper ad which lists all who contributed and includes a phrase like "These are the folks who helped make it all possible!" If it means paying for this, that is OK and worth the outlay. Just negotiate your best rate and do it.

In the rush of things, a phone call, even if it is a message left on an answering machine, is beneficial.

Fundraising letter "thank yous"

Most of the above still applies. A quick response is important. Don't wait for weeks to do this. Try and do it within a couple of days from receiving a check or pledge. Your response should include an acknowledgement of the amount, and a warm, personal sentiment of thanks for the generous gift. Remember, it is this reply that serves as their official receipt. Therefore, any letterhead used or other form of note card should include details of the tax-exempt status of the organization and the date. Note that if the fundraiser takes place at the end of the year, it may be sensitive and appropriate to ask the donor, in the case of a large gift, if he/she would like the receipt to reflect the gift in the current year or the next year.

Last points

Even businesses are people. So when acknowledging and thanking a business, find out who exactly needs to be thanked. In some cases it is just the business name itself, but in other cases, there may be an individual who also deserves credit. This may be the owner, manager, person who authorized the check or someone else. Example:

Wells Fargo Bank, Greg Majors.
Coldwell Banker Bailey and Company, Dennis Bailey.
Flairmont Furniture, Ed De Julio.

Lastly, use your own influence to encourage your board and others involved, to support these businesses. Reciprocation is a time honored tradition that exemplifies the win win strategy and makes sure that no gift is taken for granted. Indeed, many of us will never know to what lengths some givers have gone to help our cause.

Conclusion

Asking others to help is beneath no one. Expectations and results will vary. What people will give or not give provides one of the greatest opportunities to practice non-judgmentalism. Either way, thanks are due.

To get beyond the "special interest" persona that most not-for-profit organizations represent, you have to find ways of appealing to a larger segment of the local population. One way of doing this is to actively find out, through personal contacts, networking and media assistance, who else there is, out there, who shares your view. Then you have to communicate with them. Another way is to broaden the scope of the endeavor so that it embraces other groups of potential donors and beneficiaries. It is these other people who are on the periphery or well outside of your normal audience, who can make all the difference. In all cases, success will be enhanced if the project or program of work can be seen and promoted as serving the needs of more components of the community; For example, seniors, children, single parents, minorities, families, the disadvantaged, visitors, etc., convenience, accessibility and/or the nature and effectiveness of the services performed are also very important.

The need itself has to be reconcilable and made easy to sell. It should not be vague. It must have facts and figures to support it. Above all, it has to be put over in such a way that the appeal strikes the heart of other people. The person who said that you don't sell coal; you sell heat, got it right. It is always the benefits that need to be promoted.

Getting people to help you, who are willing, capable and not afraid to ask, is the key. The more people you ask, the more money you will get. Therefore, spending time on the means necessary to insure that no stone is left unturned, will always pay off.

The bigger the project and goals are, the more volunteers you will need. There is a limit to how many places of business or individuals that you can ask one or two people to contact. The maximum is probably 40 but in most cases it will be closer to 12. And remember, if presentations have to be made, especially to municipalities or boards, a team of well-qualified people is essential.

Lastly, concentrate on your own community. Unless the cause you represent is truly regional, the average person or business seldom gives to a community outside of their own immediate area. The only exceptions to this are businesses who do a significant portion of their gross sales in surrounding areas beyond their home base, and second homeowners who stand to benefit directly from what you are doing.

Anyone wishing to be effective in raising money has to be positive, optimistic and enthusiastic. If led correctly, others will follow. This becomes essential because nearly all forms of raising money require a concerted, joint effort.

And when it really comes down to it, all fundraising is about being able to motivate others to the point that they feel impelled to put their hand in their pocket

So go on out there. Ask and thou shalt receive. Guaranteed!

Some useful fundraising tools

Examples of ideas for adaptation to different situations

Fundraising Letter (School Bond)
Letterhead, fundraising letter and contribution sheet (Montrose Ute Indian Museum)
Annual Membership Letter (OPAG)
Membership cards (OPAG)
Botanical Society Appeal Letter
Botanical Society Membership appeal Envelope
A Three Part Receipt
Silent Auction Bidding Sheet
A Golf Tournament Flier
The Non Event Invitation
Jail Lock-up Warrant
Jail Lock-up Hints
Jail Lock-up "Wanted"
Jail Lock-up Bond Sheet
Endowment Trust, Methodist Church
Foundation, Montrose Education

All fundraising for anything that benefits the local community should be concentrated in that community. The only possible exceptions to this would be grant applications, solicitations to out of town businesses who trade in your community, appeals by letter to people who have two or more residences, one of which is in your own community, and to neighboring communities if the cause or service provided directly benefits a portion of that community. Each community essentially looks after itself. How many times do you give to another community?

Fundraising Letter (School Bond)

This letter was sent out to a section of the local business community. It achieved its goal and the school bond passed!

We need your help and tangible support!

The School Bond issue is in the balance. It is safe to say that the overwhelming majority of us see the need as urgent and crucial but it won't happen by itself!

All the surveys, independent analysis and current state of affairs indicate a very real need to catch up in providing the additional space and better quality of physical plant for our children. This is not about trying to outdo our competitors: it is about ensuring that we do not lag behind any further. In short, passage of a reasonably priced School Bond is long overdue.

As most of you are aware, our community has only passed one School Bond in the last 21 years. That was in 1990 and it didn't come close to addressing the needs at that time. In fact, it was a watered down version of an already bare boned list of absolute necessities.

Since then, the need has increased by a considerable amount and still has not been addressed in such a way that has produced a successful Bond Issue. This state of affairs has to change. As responsible citizens, property owners and businessmen and women, we need to act and help return the Pride in our schools and system that our community deserves.

Fundraising Letter (School Bond)

Our goal here is simply to raise the money that is needed to cover the costs of pamphlets, advertising and general promotion of this subject, mainly to assist in educating voters and showing them the reasons to say **yes**.

We will need a total of $25,000 and we need it by April 30th.

We ask you, unashamedly, to put a value on the importance of bringing our schools up to standard with no frills and no political overtones.

We do not want to place a limit on your giving preference but we hope that we can count on at least $50 to $100. To make this easier, a stamped addressed envelope is enclosed.

All of us here are committed to seeing this Bond pass by whatever way is deemed best for all. We cannot afford to let the momentum slip away and we cannot afford to fail.

For our community's sake, please respond as soon as you can. This will give us the encouragement and support we require to complete our task and get this thing moving in the right direction.

Thank you,

(Signed by "Pride Committee" co-chairs).

An example of a capital project letterhead and fundraising letter

MONTROSE UTE INDIAN MUSEUM

Enhancement and Hospitality Project

A LOCAL FUND RAISING PROJECT IN CONJUNCTION WITH THE COLORADO HISTORICAL SOCIETY

CO-CHAIRPERSONS

Tricia M. Dickinson

Kelvin B. Kent

COMMITTEE

Andy Masick
Executive Director
Colorado Historical Society

Jim Hartman
President
Colorado Historical Society

Glen Gross
Administrator
Ute Indian Museum

REPRESENTATIVES FROM THE SERVICE CLUBS OF MONTROSE

Montrose Rotary Club

Montrose Altrusa Club

Black Canyon Kiwanis Club

Noon Kiwanis Club

Evening Lions Club

Morning Lions Club

Montrose Chamber of Commerce

The Redcoats

Visitors Convention Bureau

The Friends of the Ute Museum

October 12, 1995

Dear

We realize there is always a lot going on and that this will not be the only current request for your financial support. However, we feel it is important enough for our community area to bring to your attention and ask directly for a contribution.

First of all, this is a one-time effort. Our fact sheet explains the concept and gives some of the details.

We have a wonderful opportunity to enlarge the Ute Museum, bring it up to date, put in handicap-accessible restrooms and entrance ramp, and combine it with a Visitors Information Center so that the facility can be open 12 months of the year.

The good news is that out of $285,000 necessary to complete the project, $185,000 is already in place. We (the community, friends and supporters) have to come up with the remaining $100,000.

Already, the Service Clubs have pledged their support, and over $15,000 was raised at the kickoff function on September 12. Local businesses are being asked for their support, as are some of our larger area property owners. We are also seeking grants and now have close to $30,000 in cash and pledges.

But it is our hope that a very real source of support will be from individuals like us, who traditionally come forward to support the things which will be of benefit to the community. Therefore, please take a minute to read the fact sheet and send in your contribution.

ACCOUNTING: ALL MONIES RECEIVED AND DISPENSED WILL BE CHANNELED THROUGH THE EXISTING ACCOUNT OF THE FRIENDS OF THE UTE MUSEUM WHICH IS A NOT FOR PROFIT CHARITABLE ORGANIZATION SET UP UNDER SEC. 501 C(3). CHECKS SHOULD BE WRITTEN TO "FRIENDS OF THE UTE MUSEUM".

ADDRESS: FRIENDS OF THE UTE MUSEUM · BOX 652 · MONTROSE, COLORADO 81402

TELEPHONE: (970) 249-3098 (MUSEUM) OR (970) 249-2451 (KELVIN KENT)

An example of a capital project letterhead and fundraising letter

We thank you in advance for your support, and know that the finished product will be attractive, educational, and of great benefit to our community and visitors alike. This can happen because of your efforts and contributions.

The groundbreaking and Ute Blessing Ceremony took place on September 23 at the museum and was a great success. Please now help us turn this wonderful project into a beneficial reality!

Sincerely,

Tricia M. Dickinson　　　Kelvin B. Kent

Co-Chairpersons, Fundraising Committee

P.S. This is how we got the Pavilion, the Magic Circle Theater, the new Chamber building, the Academic Booster Club, the Airport Terminal Building, the Aquatic Center, passage of the School Bonds, the Criminal Justice Complex and the Library, and that's why Montrose is the outstanding community and place to live that it is!

P.P.S. None of the money received in this appeal will be used for administrative expenses. All materials, time, typing and postage have already been donated and will cost us nothing.

Contribution/Pledge Sheet

CONTRIBUTION OR PLEDGE

I/we ______________________________

support the Montrose Ute Indian Museum Enhancement and Hospitality Project

and are pleased to contribute $__________ (dollar amount).

We enclose our check made payable to "Friends of the Ute Museum," or

We pledge a total of $________ (dollar amount).

Name(s) (print) ______________________

Address: ______________________

____

Signed______________________Date:__________

CONTRIBUTION LEVELS

*Brave	$1 to $25
*Warrior	$26 to $99
*Chief	$100 to $250
*Chief of all the Utes	$251 to $500
*Ute Guardian	$501 to $1,000
*Ute Patron	$1,000 to 2,500
*Ute Benefactor	Over $2,500

No matter what the size of your contribution, anything received will be most gratefully accepted and will help us achieve our goal. Receipts will be given and all contributions will be tax deductible. Please send direct to:

Friends of the Ute Museum
P.O. Box 652
Montrose, CO 81402

An annual membership letter

Ouray Performing Arts Guild, Inc. P.O. Box 14, Ouray, CO 81427

Dear OPAG Friend and supporter,

It is with great pleasure that we address this report to you. In the last 18 months, thanks to people and businesses like you, we have come a long way and your current Board of Directors feels very good at what is happening

Since the middle of last year, we have erased a debt of over $9000 and broken even on the 2002 "Music In Ouray" festival This was achieved because of extra strong fundraising efforts and response to our need by so many of our fine local businesses and individual supporters.

As most of you know, we have decided that the effort involved and costs associated with bringing the Raphael Trio and supporting artists to Ouray (over $30,000), are just too excessive to maintain on an annual basis and therefore, we will not be presenting "Music in Ouray" with the Raphael Trio again. Nevertheless, we will be pursuing several top quality performers and events, including more Sunday Salons, designed to make the 2003 season the best ever.

We are most proud of what has been accomplished in the last year and here are some of the highlights:

- Ouray Annual Christmas Variety Show.
- Mesa State Faculty Brass Quintet concert.
- Music in Ouray series.
- Salon featuring Erin Kenedy and Gaby Larkin: Dramatic reading and Interpretive movement.
- Salon featuring Maureen Sorenson and Nancy Ziglar: Soprano soloist and accompaniest.
- Salon featuring James Davis: Classical Guitar.
- Salon featuring Jill Olsen: Concert pianist.
- Salon featuring Chameleon Ensemble: Christine Embree, Jane Holmes and Nancy Ziglar
- David Taylor Dance Theater.
- Wilson McKee Folk and Celtic concert.
- Collaboration with Montrose Arts Council for Telluride Wintersing Concert on December 7th at Montrose Methodist Church (2pm).
- Move of the concert grand piano from the Wright Opera House to Ouray school and the move of the school's smaller grand piano to Bill and Judith Allred's house where it can be used by OPAG. [cost $1000!]
- Two performing arts events for the benefit of Ridgway and Ouray school students

In order to expand the scope, quality and quantity of good events, we need to build up a reasonable fund which can help underwrite individual performances. Traditionally and Statistically ticket income for performing arts events seldom accounts for more than 30% of the cost of the event.

With this letter is a card with our statement of purpose, combined with a new annual membership structure for 2003. <u>We urge you to review it and show your support by filling it in and sending it back to us by the end of the year.</u> The actual amount you chose to give is not so important as the gesture it conveys, although we do hope that some will be able to contribute at higher levels

Lastly, your Board, which has expanded nicely since the summer, is committed to working hard and doing their best to promote the finest performing arts for all of this county. Together we can succeed!

Most sincerely,

Sue Hillhouse President and Kelvin Kent Vice President

Board of Directors: Sue Hillhouse, President, Kelvin Kent, Vice President, Tom Hillhouse, Secretary, Jim Francis, Treasurer Sara Sharpe Gillis, Linda Hoedsema, Becky Lindsay-Kent, Virginia Bellows, Don Reed, Criss Bartley, Bev Anselm, Jorg Angehrn, Carol Kline

Membership Cards

Yes! I want to do my part to help the performing arts prosper in Ouray & Ridgway.

Name

Mailing Address

City State Zip

Phone (Home) (Business)

Business Name (if a business membership)

E-Mail Address

Yearly Membership - Individual/Family

- ☐ Individual ($25)
- ☐ Family ($35)
- ☐ Patron of the Arts ($50 or more)
- ☐ Supporting Patron ($100 or more)
- ☐ Benefactor ($250 or more)

Patrons' and Benefactors' names will be printed in our programs

Yearly Membership - Business

- ☐ Business ($50)
- ☐ Business Patron ($100)
- ☐ Benefactor ($250 or more)

Patrons' and Benefactors' names will be printed in our programs.

☐ I am interested in being a volunteer or serving on the board. Please contact me.

Suggestions for programs and/or activities I would like to see the Ouray Performing Arts Guild sponsor

Please make your check payable to OPAG

Return to:
OPAG
P.O. Box 14
Ouray, CO 81427

Membership and gift contributions are tax deductible within IRS guidelines

Ouray Performing Arts Guild, Inc.

P.O. Box 14
Ouray, Colorado 81427

Purpose

The Ouray Performing Arts Guild is a non profit organization established to promote a broad spectrum of performing arts at different locations within Ouray County, at affordable prices.

Goals

To bring performing artists of high caliber to our area.

To encourage local performing artists and help support them.

To provide education about the performing arts and generate enthusiasm for their support.

To assist with school programs which include music, dance and other modes of artistic performance.

To host a series of Salons which showcase local or imported talent in an atmosphere of intimacy and social interaction.

To act as custodian of both Grand pianos and utilize their availability to promote musical events.

To support the concept of having a suitable performing arts center in the county.

Your Part

We are a small volunteer group dependent upon your membership and strong support of our efforts to enhance the cultural environment within Ouray county.

We are therefore asking everybody who considers performing arts to be an important ingredient in our community lifestyle, to step forward and show that support by becoming a member at the highest level that you can. This show of participation and tangible [illegible] support will indicate to the board your level of [illegible] and give us the resources to proceed.

In grateful recognition of your Membership dues and contributions, we will include your names and businesses at the Patron level and above, in all of our printed programs. We also plan to hold one special event to which all members at the Supporting Patron level ($100 and above) will receive a special invitation.

Please see the reverse side and respond without delay. Thank you.

An excellent fundraising letter

Montrose Botanical Society

March 13, 2003

Mr. and Mrs. Kelvin Kent
1144 Ridge
Montrose, CO 81401

Dear Becky and Kelvin:

The Montrose Botanical Society, stewards of the Montrose Botanic Gardens, needs your pledge of support in the development of the **Xeriscape Demonstration Garden**. After the past couple of years of drought conditions, it is quite appropriate that the Botanical Society focus its efforts this year towards developing a xeric-oriented garden that will demonstrate water conservation techniques through educational displays, drip irrigation, the use of non-thirsty plants and turf and appropriate mulch. We believe that there is a need to educate the community about conserving water in landscapes, especially in these drought conditions.

Towards the challenge of completing this one-half acre Xeriscape Garden as scheduled, we are in the midst of an intensive fund raising drive. Our goal is to raise the necessary $75,000 through local support and charitable organizations. As a local non-profit organization, the Montrose Botanical Society has found in the past that the most successful fund raising campaigns have been accomplished by garnering support from those who will immediately benefit from our efforts. Those benefactors are you, the local citizens of the Montrose and Uncompahgre Valley area.

How can you help? There are two ways you can help with the development of the Xeriscape Demonstration Garden.

- Firstly, direct a letter of support to the Montrose Botanical Society expressing your support either as an organization or individual. This show of support will be effective in soliciting grant moneys from other organizations and groups that help fund botanical garden projects. As we are aggressive in our project schedule, I am hoping your letter could reach us by the end of this month.
- Secondly, pledge a monetary support. We know that several $500 and $100 pledges will take us closer to accomplishing our goal. Your pledge will be prominently recognized for all to appreciate within the Xeriscape Demonstration Garden. Your charitable support of the Montrose Botanical Society is considered a tax deductible contribution.

Either or both of the above gestures go a long way in supporting this project.

Please do not hesitate to give me a call as I am always available to present more information about this and the other projects that we have completed over the past four years. You can reach me at my office at 249-5404 or at home 240-9236.

Thank you.

John Eloe, Board Member
Montrose Botanical Society

PS
I am enclosing a copy of the Montrose Botanic Garden master plan with an indication of where the Xeriscape Demonstration Garden will be located.

"A Demonstration Garden"
P.O. Box 323 • Montrose, Colorado 81402 • 970-249-0742

A Membership Envelope

All of this is printed on the inside back cover of the envelope, which has a fold-down leaf.

The outside of the fold-down back leaf cover has an attractive borderline of flowers with a note saying: Thank you for supporting Montrose Botanic Gardens.

Montrose Botanical Society

Your membership contribution is important!

Please check membership level

- ☐ Naturalist (Senior/Student) $15.00
- ☐ Gardener (Individual) $20.00
- ☐ Roots & Shoots (Family) $30.00
- ☐ Botany Club $50.00 - $200.00
- ☐ Alpine Club $200.00 - $500.00
- ☐ Garden Angel $500.00 - $1000.00
- ☐ Visionary $1000.00 and above

Please circle the following areas in which you are interested.

Horticulture: Planting, Weeding
Public Relations: Newsletter, Booth sitting, Programs
Membership: Phone Tree, Mailing
Special events: Plant Sale, etc.
Master Plan: Fund Raising, Capital Improvements, Grant Writing.

Our gardens and programs are funded entirely through the generosity of our donors.

(This is the line of the fold of the envelope)
Below is the text for the actual back of the envelope. as you would see it having lifted up the overlap fold that has the info shown above.

Make checks payable to Montrose Botanical Society. Gifts are tax deductible with IRS guidelines.

New membership/Renewal Membership
Name(s) ______________________________
Address ______________________________
City, State, Zip __________________________

Send gift membership to:
Name(s)______________________________
Address______________________________
City, State, Zip__________________________
Gift Card Signed_________________________

Fence Fund Donation
For only $20.00 per foot, you will be a "Fence Fund Friend." I have enclosed $__________ for __________ ft. of fencing.

I would like my donation to be in honor of

____

Or in memory of ___________________

A Three Part Auction Receipt

IN KIND DONATION

☐ Hospice of the Grand Valley
2754 Compass Dr., Suite 377
Grand Junction, CO 81506
(970) 241-2212 • Fax (970) 257-2400

☐ Hospice of the Plateau Valley
P.O. Box 294
Collbran, CO 81624
(970) 487-3061

☐ Hospice of the Uncompahgre Valley
P.O. Box 1804
Montrose, CO 81402
(970) 240-7734 • Fax (970) 240-726

Date___/___/__

Item(s) Donated and Description ______________________________

____

____

Estimated Value $ __________________

It is the privilege and right of the donor to place a value on items being donated to Hospice.

Donated by ____
Business Name Contact

Address ____
Street / P.O. Box

____
City State Zip Phone

Hospice Representative __________________

Silent Auction Bidding Sheet

(Name of Your Orgnization Here)

GOLF PACKAGE

Two rounds of 18 holes with 3 new balls for two people with cart.

Donated By: GOLF CLUB

Value
$_____

Minimm Bid/Reserve Price
$_____

Bidder Name, Tele, Amount		Bidder Name, Tele, Amount	
Jhon Doe, 111-1111	*$$*		

[Bidding increments are to be no less than $5]

Golf Tournament Flier

hospice and palliative care

5TH ANNUAL
HOSPICE GOLF TOURNAMENT

SPONSORED BY
CRIPPIN FUNERAL HOME

Black Canyon Golf Course, Montrose, Colo.
Saturday, June 14th, 2003
9:00 AM Shotgun Start
Ladies & Men - 4 person team scramble
any combination can play

*Mulligans Available *** Teams Will Be Flighted*
1st, 2nd & 3rd Places will be paid in each flight
$80.00 per Player, includes Cart, Shirt & Buffet
PLEASE JOIN US FOR FUN, GREAT GOLF,
AND LOTS OF FABULOUS PRIZES

TEAM NAME ______________________ PHONE #____________

Player Names	Shirt Size	Handicap
1. ______________________	______	______
2. ______________________	______	______
3. ______________________	______	______
4. ______________________	______	______

Please mail entry forms and entry fees to
Hospice & Palliative Care of Western Colorado
P.O. Box 1804, Montrose, CO 81402
For more information, call Greg or Rex 249-2121

ALL PROCEEDS BENEFIT HOSPICE

The Non-Event Invitation

You are cordially invited…

…To spend a quiet night at home with your family, with a good book, with a funny movie…

Founded in 1912 by a group of volunteer dentists, KIND provides affordable, comprehensive dental care to children from families with low incomes. Families are asked to pay a small portion of the costs, but no child is turned away due to inability to pay.

During 2000, KIND provided $1.56 million worth of dental services, including $389,000 worth of care donated by volunteer dental professionals.

KIND is the oldest dental charity in the country and the first to earn the endorsement of the American Dental Association.

For more information, please visit KIND's web site at: www.kindsmiles.org.

The Non-Event Invitation

As you plan your busy Holiday schedule, designate one evening just for you – to spend however you like, courtesy of Kids in Need of Dentistry (KIND).

We know you can come up with a better way to spend an evening than to attend another after-hours event, but we still count on your generosity during this time of year...

Your tax-deductible gift to KIND will have value throughout the year to thousands of children in need. For example:

- *A $1,000 gift pays for a part-time KIND dentist to work 3.5 days and provide approximately $6,500 worth of dental services*
- *A $500 gift can provide preventive sealants to protect 1,163 molars against decay*
- *A $250 gift can be used to buy new toothbrushes for 1,000 children*
- *A gift of mutual funds, stock or other securities can provide untold value to young patients in need of dental care. (Contact Nancy Schoyer at 303-733-2119 for more information).*

Enclosed is a donation card you can submit with your gift.
R.S.V.P.s are not necessary, but feel free to call us at 303-733-3710 if you <u>want</u> to attend another party or would like information on what KIND is doing right now to give more Colorado kids healthy smiles.

Jail Lock-up Warrant

THIS IS A WARRANT FOR YOUR ARREST

YOU'VE BEEN CHARGED WITH AIDING AND ABETTING A LOCAL CHARITY WITH THE INTENT OF HELPING TO FIGHT THE CRIME OF NEUROMUSCULAR DISEASES.

September 09, 2002

Kelvin Kent
1144 Ridge
Montrose, CO 81401

Dear Kelvin,

Congratulations!!!! As one of MDA's "Most Wanted," you've been chosen to be locked up for "GOOD" Tuesday, September 24 at Backwoods Inn. You will turn yourself into the MDA Jail at 2:00 PM for the Montrose Lock-Up.

Your bail has been set at $1,050, which sends 2 kids to MDA Summer Camp. We've enclosed several items to help you. Photocopy the "Most Wanted" Flyer and Fax sheet to mail or fax to all of your associates, vendors and friends. **Don't forget to follow up with a personal phone call!**

By participating in this event, you're making a difference in the fight against neuromuscular disease. Your "Bail Money" will help support thousands of individuals affected by muscular dystrophy by providing clinic services, support groups, research grants and the Colorado summer camp program.

All we ask is that you have fun raising your bail . . . the more fun you have the more successful you will be. If you have any questions, please don't hesitate to give me a call at 719/260-8777.

See you in Jail,

Kim Bruna
MDA Warden

Jail Lock-up Hints

HINTS TO HELP YOU RAISE YOUR BAIL

1. Begin raising your bail right away!!! The earlier, the easier!

2. Suggest a minimum of $100 from businesses and $25 donations from individuals.

3. Fax and Email your accounts and business contact with the enclosed flyers prior to the event and ask them to make a donation on your behalf.
   It's proven, these flyers are the key to reaching your bail!

4. Does your company have matching funds? Ask those you receive donations from to ask their employers about matching funds also.

5. Post the enclosed flyers with your picture in a visible area at your work place. You'll be amazed at the attention it creates and the bail you'll generate.

6. Be creative! Your ideas can help to generate enthusiasm in others to contribute towards your bail.

7. Collect your donations before the Lock-Up! Bring in your whole bail in cash or checks and receive an MDA Lock-Up T-shirt and chance at the Grand Prize!!!

THANK YOU AND GOOD LUCK !!!

Muscular Dystrophy Association, 5350 Tomah Drive, Ste 1800, Colorado Springs, CO 80918 (719) 260-8777 Fax (71) 260-9443

Jail Lock-up "Wanted"

TO:	FAX:	PHONE:
FROM: Kelvin Kent	FAX:	PHONE: 970/249-6468

MDA LOCK-UP

WANTED

DESCRIPTION: **Usually Wears A Smile . . .**
CAUTION: **Heavily Armed With Kindness . . . This Could Be Contagious**
PRIOR CONVICTION: **Thoughtfulness and Generosity**

Please Help Me!!! I've been arrested and will be put in jail for the **Montrose Lock-up to benefit the Muscular Dystrophy Association**. Don't even bother asking what crime I've committed – it's not really important. I just have to raise my bail of **$1,050 (which will send 2 kids to MDA Summer Camp)** ***before*** the Backwoods Inn Lock-Up and they'll go easy on me, but I need ***your*** financial assistance to post my bond.

Your 100 percent tax-deductible donation will help MDA continue research into the causes of and cures for 43 neuromuscular diseases. Your support of the MDA Lock-Up will also help MDA provide wheelchairs, clinic visits and summer camp for people in our local area.

YOU CAN MAIL YOUR DONATIONS TO ME AT (**Check made payable to MDA**):

____

____

I WISH TO DONATE : $106 ____ (2 Research Minutes) $75 ____ (1 Day at Camp) $53 ____ (1 Research Minute)

$ ______ IF THEY PROMISE TO KEEP YOU!!!! ($525 sends a child to MDA Summer Camp!)

____ PAYMENT ENCLOSED

____ CHARGE IT! ____ VISA ____ MC ____ AMEX ____ DISC

ACCOUNT NUMBER ______________ EXP. DATE ______________

NAME ______________ PHONE NUMBER ______________

COMPANY ______________

ADDRESS ______________

____

____

I MUST HAVE ALL MY BAIL MONEY BY Monday, September 23, SO PLEASE HELP ME NOW!!!

Jail Lock-up Bond Sheet

Muscular Dystrophy Association

5350 Tomah Drive, Suite 1800
Colorado Springs, CO 80918
(719) 260-8777

Lock-Up Bond Sheet

Jailbird: ____________________ Company: ____________________

Address: ____________________ Phone: ____________________

Please Use This Form For To Record Cash and Checks Collected Prior To This Event. Make Checks payable to MDA

Sponsor's Name	Street Address	City	Zip Code	Phone	Amount Paid
					$
					$
					$
					$
					$
					$
					$
					$
					$
					$
					$
					$
					$
					$
					$
					$
					$
					$
					$
					$
Bail $1050			Total		$

Endowment Trust, Methodist Church

The First United Methodist Church of Montrose

ENDOWMENT TRUST

Established in March 1998 and approved at the 1998 Church/Change Conference

Providing opportunities for charitable giving; separate from, and over and above, annual Church operating budget pledges, through out-right gifts of money, memorials, insurance proceeds, property and stocks and bonds, both now, in one's lifetime, or later, through wills, bequests and estate planning.

Endowment Trust, Methodist Church

FURTHER INFORMATION

This Trust has been established using guidelines provided by the United Methodist Church Book of Discipline, The Rocky Mountain Conference and the Council on Finance and Administration of the United Methodist Church and its Affiliated Organization in Evanston, Illinois and in accordance with established rules of the Internal Revenue Service covering exemption from federal income tax under section 501(c)(3) of the Code.

ADMINISTRATION OF TRUST

This Endowment Trust is administered by a separate, six-person Board of Trustees, appointed by the Church to fulfill terms not exceeding three years. The Board itself elects a Chairperson, Vice-Chairperson, Secretary and Treasurer.

Trustees of our Endowment Trust will be happy to talk with you further regarding any questions or help you may require in connection with your stewardship decision. Please contact the Church at 249-3716 or any of the duly appointed trustees.

We thank you for reading this and hope that you may be able to include this special opportunity in your planned giving arrangements.

Endowment Trust, Methodist Church

Purpose and Function of the Trust

Our Methodist Church here in Montrose is a building of significant architectural interest. The Church's beauty, strength, and design is unique to the area. But even more important than that is our function as a growing, enthusiastic and highly effective Christian congregation whose leadership and pastoral staff provide an ever increasing level of Ministry, ready to take us into the twenty-first century.

Each year a Church budget is put together to cater for all of our work areas, administrative expenses and outreach ministries. This annual amount sustains the day to day operations of our church, but does not build for the future.

The establishment of this Endowment Trust provides for income to be wisely invested and allowed to grow over the years. Only the interest from the Trust can be spent, leaving the principal to increase. This endeavor will assure the long term health and viability of our church in cases of emergency or poorer times, and contribute towards other important aspects of our ministry.

Gifts to the Trust may be classified as designated or undesignated. Designated gifts shall be in the amount of not less that $2,000.00 Undesignated gifts may be in any amount.

Endowment Trust, Methodist Church

It is the intent of the Board of Trustees that the following main categories be set up initially to help provide areas of disbursement:

A) Mission Fund- for missions in and beyond the local church and community

B) Building Fund- for maintenance, care, improvement, and construction of physical plant and facilities

C) General Fund: for special needs and ministries determined by the Church Council

D) Other areas of need as deemed advisable in the course of time.

At the end of each year, accrued interest may be spent to assist needs within the categories shown above, leaving the principle intact.

Foundation, Montrose Education

Foundation, Montrose Education

Dear Supporter of Education.

The Montrose Education Foundation was created in 1995 for the purpose of supporting and enhancing educational opportunities for the students of Montrose District RE-1J. It is the objective of the Foundation to provide this support by building and maintaining a permanent fund, the earnings of which will be used to achieve the Foundation's purpose. To this end, the by-laws of the Foundation provide that any contribution greater than $1,000 can only be added to the permanent fund. In this way, the resources of the Foundation will grow perpetually and be available to provide an ongoing and continuous source of assistance for the young people of the Olathe and Montrose communities as they seek educational opportunities.

The Foundation is managed by an active board of directors and is guided and supported by a large honorary board of directors. The people who serve on the various boards represent a cross-section of residents in the Montrose and Olathe communities, and are dedicated to the purpose and the long term success of the Foundation. If you are interested in serving on either the active or honorary boards, please let us know.

The Foundation has applied for and received tax exempt status under Section 501(c)(3) of the Internal Revenue Code, and all contributions to the foundation are therefore deductible for income tax purposes. The Foundation targets both current and future donors in its fundraising efforts, seeking current contributions through various programs, solicitations and future contributions by asking people to consider the Foundation in their long range gift and estate planning. The Foundation is also developing an alumni directory of graduates of the RE-1J schools as a source of regular support.

Education is our future, and the Foundation is dedicated to the long term support of the educational opportunities for the young people of our communities. With your help, the Foundation can grow and have a positive impact for this generation and all generations to come.

Thank you for your support.

Sincerely,

DENNIS R. DEVOR
Montrose Education Foundation, Inc.
President

MISSION STATEMENT

The Montrose Education Foundation is a community-based advocate for quality education for all children in the RE-1J Schools in the Olathe and Montrose areas. The purpose of the Foundation shall be to:

* promote understanding and interaction between RE-1J schools and the community
* encourage innovative thinking to enable schools and the District to meet the challenges of the future
* secure resources from individuals, school alumni, corporations, businesses, and foundations to support programs
* support technology efforts in our schools that foster better teaching and learning
* assist young people, primarily preschool through high school, in their educational endeavors, including the encouragement of academic and artistic excellence and creativity
* promote school alumni
* administer and provide scholarships to youth for academic and vocational pursuits

About the Author

Kelvin Kent was born on the Island of Jersey, trained in London and spent 17 years in the British Army, serving in Europe, Africa, and Asia. He has participated in several major expeditions including, overland journeys from UK to India, Alaska to Chile, and climbs of Annapurna and Everest. He came to the US in 1976 and successfully operated a small business until 2000. For the last 30 years he has helped lead dozens of fundraisers in his own community. He is the author of two local hiking guides and now lives in Ouray Colorado, with his wife Becky.